FULLY INVESTED

Improv explains the world of money, and vice-versa

By Laurie R. Kauffman

Illustrations by T. Scheirer

First edition published 2010 by Barclay Bryan Press
Second edition published 2011 by Net Worth Publishing

Printed in the United States of America
ISBN 978-0-6155221-0-4

Critical Praise for FULLY INVESTED:

I thoroughly enjoyed **Fully Invested**. It is provocative, funny, revealing, informative, and just plain fun to read. I am coming from a place where I know a lot about finance and absolutely nothing about improv. The parallels are remarkable. Kauffman's vivid illustrations of financial concepts are wonderful; the value of the never-worn celery suit bought on sale in her asset utilization discussion is perfect. Since finishing the book I find myself thinking about different parts, smiling and looking forward to taking in some improv soon.

VP of major financial services firm who must remain anonymous.

Improv isn't about knowing what to do, it's about being comfortable in not knowing. It shakes us from the safe sameness of our daily lives and helps us see ourselves, our world and our choices anew. Laurie's book draws unique parallels between improv and finance, and encourages us to fail and fear and find comfort in the unknown, to make us stronger versions of ourselves.

Christian Capozzoli, improviser, writer, instructor and author of ***Aerodynamics of Yes – The Improviser's Manual.***

In improvisation the name of the game is making the unreal real through intent. The improviser's goal is to make the other player look good and to feel safe in unsettling circumstances. Discovering that the same forms we use onstage to make something out of nothing also apply to the financial world is a welcome revelation.

Jeff Michalski, distinguished artist, innovator, and teacher, and former director of Chicago's ***Second City.***

Laurie cuts a unique approach explaining financial choice through her personal experiences with improvisational comedy. It's brassy, quick paced and entertaining.

Terry Wells, long-time global leader in sales and business development

How brilliant -- marrying the concept of improv and money gave me a clearer understanding of how they work together and how to operate on my own financial stage! Laurie Kauffman's witty look into the world of money and improv will be a unique guide for making smarter financial decisions. As a small business owner in Washington, DC, I found it an empowering resource in connecting the finance lessons to the real life money. My retail operation has thrived using these principles.

Jackie Flanagan, owner of Nana (voted Best Boutique by ***The Washington City Paper*** *in both 2010 and 2011.)*

For anyone who's ever found the world of finance to be abstract and intimidating, **Fully Invested** is the perfect guide for understanding all things money-related. While Laurie Kauffman's book is full of useful ideas and principles it is also profoundly human; her insights into how we live are firmly rooted in real life as we live it. Kauffman's personality shines through every line. Reading this book is like sitting down for a coffee with a good friend who will not only break it all down for you, but also make you laugh, challenge you to think in new ways, and empower you to go out and live more fully. I've had such chats with Laurie Kauffman and her words have been a great help in running my non-profit theater. **Fully Invested** is an opportunity for everyone to spend some eye-opening quality time with Laurie.

Steven Cosson is the Artistic Director of New York-based theater company The Civilians.

To the two best bad financial decisions
I ever made, my sons Zakkai and Ezra,
who were improvised with love.

Contents

Introduction
Improv and Finance: Follow the Fear 1

Chapter One
How To Win Money Fights
With Your Significant Other 21

Chapter Two
Send My Spinach To China 35

Chapter Three
Is Having Kids a Good Financial Move?
Performing Improv? 44

Chapter Four
Should You Pick Up the Check? 54

Chapter Five
The Answer Is (Drumroll Please!) ...
$150,000! 66

Chapter Six
Kill the Cars 76

Chapter Seven
Should You Give a Mouse a Cookie? 87

Chapter Eight
Is Running a Non-Profit a Good Career Move? What About an Improv Troupe? *97*

Chapter Nine
Ten Things You Need To Know To Look Smart About Money *110*

Afterword *134*

Introduction

Improv and Finance: Follow The Fear

How would you like to sign up for something that will publicly reveal the deepest truths about you, force you to relinquish control to others, and - most likely - fail?

Welcome to the fields of improvisational comedy and finance! They have an amazing amount in common. Taking a shot at success in either one is well worth the humiliation and probable terror.

Most people, when faced with fear, try to avoid it or pretend it's not real. The racing heart, sweaty brow, and narrowing field of vision are not at all pleasant. Admitting you're afraid is not exactly high on the list of standard confidence-builders. In fact, admitting you have any feelings at all can tank your career (ask Edmund Muskie).

This book is based on the concept of not only acknowledging fear, but actually letting it lead. On a good day, I try to view my fear as a kindly tour guide, unveiling vistas of uncharted adventures. On a bad day, I use my fear to get my rear end in gear.

My philosophies of life are: *If you're not getting rejected four times a day you're not trying hard enough;* and *The reward of the struggle is the opportunity to struggle.*

I am not masochistic. I do finance and improv together and separately because the opportunity to struggle yields amazing results. Following the twisty roads of fear inherent in these two endeavors attracts highly interesting fellow travelers. Even better, inspiration, that elusive force, becomes a baked-in part of the journey. Inspiration fuels creativity, originality, and just plain stamina to navigate the disappointments, betrayals, and bad luck in all of our lives. The way I spend, save, waste, and invest my money mirrors this search for inspiration. Every day I get stronger and braver financially, no matter what the Dow or the deficit or my clients decide to do. Every time I perform, something good happens.

Turns out it's pretty interesting, and frequently funny, to watch somebody else struggle.

Last night was rough for our improv troupe, Third Beat. We're a small group of aspiring comics with day jobs who get together to train and perform. We have one IT technical trainer, a science writer, a former elephant trainer turned procurement professional, a non-profit strategist, a lawyer, and me.

Washington, DC is having the hottest summer on record. We'd just had not one but two apocalyptic thunderstorms which did nothing to mitigate the heat and humidity. Even the alfresco dining places were empty. Given the teaser drink prices, that was really saying something.

Our venue is philosophically perfect but physically not so much. It is long and so narrow that there is not only no backstage but also no wings. This is challenging, because improv scenes can involve any combination of the six of us. People are always "standing by" to see if they are needed. In our case there is standing alright, but not a hint of "by."

Worse, the place is an oven. It does have some funky AC and fans but they are collectively too loud to perform over and don't really work anyway. We all showed up, though, ready but not without trepidation.

Then we had to fight with the Samba group who uses the space just before we do. They only had a couple of people but still refused to leave on time. This meant that we had no place to warm up other than the alley. Between thunderstorms.

When the Samba dancers did finally deign to step-ball-change themselves out of there, we opened the doors wide, set up the chairs, and got started. The only person in the audience was my husband, who was, shall we say, not in an über-creative mood. Given all of the demotivating hassles, we did not expect to have a great show. We expected to fail.

Court Failure!

There is no Hippocratic-type oath in either improv or finance. Rather, the operating principles are *"Buyer Beware,"* and *"Past Performance Does Not Guarantee Future Results."* This is because, as I said before, both improv and finance usually fail.

Improv fails because the actors are too busy trying to be funny, are not present in the moment, and are not willing or able to reveal their true humanity and bring it out in their scene partners.

Trying to be funny doesn't work because the audience can tell you are showing off at the group's expense. While they may appreciate your rapier wit and willingness to be wacky, offensive, physically weird, or just plain bizarre, they will not fundamentally relate. The goal is always to make your scene partner look good. I read a story about an improviser who received an award. He said that he probably shouldn't accept because if his work stood out from the rest of the group's he was not doing his job. It's a paradox: the group is only as good as the individuals in it but if any one individual stands out it hurts the group.

Being present in the moment with one's head, heart, and body is nothing less than a quest for enlightenment, and as such pretty tough to pull off on command. Well nigh impossible in an oven with only one audience member. Unlike scripted performance where the actor attempts to inhabit the director's vision of the author's work, in improv you are just plain old you. All of your sterling qualities show - as does everything else. Every character you play represents some aspect of...you! The only way to get better is to become more and more authentic. The harder you try the worse you perform. If that sounds scary, it is! But the upside is that you are more and more authentic. If only for a few hours a week!

However, successful improv requires overcoming still yet another challenge: supporting your team members to be their full selves. There are techniques and formats to facilitate this but no one thing always works. The only sure way is to relax, really listen, and be open to the full range of human experience.

Finance fails because there is no reliable way to beat the market, as *we are the market*. It fails because success requires tradeoffs, and it fails because the whole thing is loaded with fear and guilt. Worst of all, like improv, the state of our finances reflects who we are. In both cases, we are naked in the wind.

Finance and values are two sides of the same coin. Just like we are what we eat, we are what we spend, save, waste, or invest. It all shows.

I decided to write this book because most financial guides implicitly and explicitly tell the reader that the reason they are failing is because there is something wrong with them. The field as a whole preys on people's all-too-present terror about our security and self-worth and fear of the future. Our lack of information is exploited for others' financial gain.

Failure is inevitable, so we may as well accept it. The cool thing is that any progress, no matter how small, toward aligning our finances with our values, is inherently both positive and sustainable. The better we get at improv, the better we'll get at finance, and, believe it or not, the opposite is also true.

Mistakes Are Opportunities

In improv we try to see our mistakes as opportunities and work them into the show. Hearteningly, they can become the best things in it. Like the Sioux, we try to use all parts of the buffalo. In finance, making money is frequently about capitalizing on the mistakes of others.

At a recent festival we asked the audience for a word to inspire us. We tried to prime the pump by soliciting the topic of a private conversation happening in a public place. One guy belted out "grenade." This was clearly a mistake. The shouter was either not listening to our question, didn't care, or was just trying to mess us up. Which happens.

One of our troupe members used this mistake by making the first line of our first scene, "I wasn't expecting *that!*" The audience, having heard both our ask and the strange response, felt the exact same way and couldn't help but laugh.

Many financial advisors, who can be helpful when working in partnership with you, measure their success against "the market." Since we are all collectively "the market," the only way to do better than the herd is to hunt for mistakes and exploit them. If one believes in the efficient market theory, which is essentially that the market always has perfect information, then the only opportunities to beat the market are to get information faster than others, take action faster, know what information is important - or change the nature of what "information" is. For example, some people believe that the best predictor of where stocks will go are women's hemlines. Up is good and down is bad. Who remembers the midi-skirt?

Others think that the Dow will go up when the NFC wins the Super Bowl. One theory says that tickers that are funny (tickers are the shortened names, originally used to describe stocks over teletype machines) presage higher stock prices than those which are boring. Take YUM, for Pizza Hut's parent company, LUV for Southwest Airlines, or BID for Sotheby's. Still others believe in the Random Walk theory which is, simply put, nobody really knows anything. How reassuring, right?

Making money in finance only happens when somebody finds places where one man's meat is another man's poison. When somebody finds a "mistake" where information is not perfect and takes a risk to act upon it. In the movie *Trading Places*, Eddie Murphy ends up working for Duke and Duke, an old-line brokerage run by Randolph and Mortimer Duke. He finds out they are bribing the Department of Agriculture to get advance notice of the state of the Florida orange crop. Eddie (whose character is named Billy Ray Valentine) learns he is the subject of a nature vs. nurture bet between the Duke brothers. Once the experiment has finished he will be dumped back on the street. Literally. When we first meet him he is begging while lying on his stomach, scooting along on a dolly pretending to be legless.

Eddie decides to double-cross his double-crossers. He intercepts the real Department of Agriculture report, which says that the orange crop is fine, and slips the Duke Brothers a fake one proclaiming that this year's crop has been decimated by bad weather. When they receive the fake report in a dark parking garage, the Duke brothers immediately try to capitalize on the market gap and buy up all the orange futures they can. (A "future" is a contract written in the present that gives buyers and sellers the option to do business in the future.) Since the Dukes thought oranges were going to be in short supply, they committed to buy them all, agreeing to pay very high prices to control the orange market.

Because the mistake in the markets they were trying to exploit was a lie, the evil bad guys got stuck using up all of their money to buy a lot of very overpriced oranges. Which they ended up having to sell at very low prices to, you guessed it, Billy Ray.

Begin With an "Ask"

Just like Billy Ray begging from his dolly, finance also begins with an "ask." One person is trying to get another to part with his money. Just like in improv, it helps if the solicitation is creative, easily understood, and trending toward the positive. We would never, for example, call for a disgusting illness or a recent incident of genocide. Implicit in both improv and financial "asks" are promises.

"Cancel up to 23 years of your mortgage!"

"Get $48,000 to pay off other bills and not have to worry about repaying that money!"

"Wouldn't you like to own your own vacation house?"

Finance promises you have a decent chance to get back more than you put in. Improv promises that everything the audience sees is completely made up on the spot just for them. The funny comes when improvisers represent real life the way it should be. The audience laughs in recognition of their own struggles writ large by people who are willing to fail but just might succeed.

Improv shows always begin with some sort of solicitation or "ask" from the audience. This brings them into the show by making them honorary troupe members and engenders trust that we really are making it up as we go along. One cardinal rule is that you have to use whatever the audience gives you, quickly and enthusiastically. Like *"grenade."* Our ask again last night was, "What is the topic of a private conversation you would not like to have in a public place?" My husband helpfully offered "rectal itch." Thank-you-very-much, dear!

Let's Get Physical

Improvisers must create believable physical realities which help to describe their characters' realities. The esteemed Mick Napier, author of *Improvise,* says that the key differentiator between a good improviser and a great one is that great ones are always fidgeting with something, just like real people do all the time.

While there is planning in terms of a structure in improv, there is no planning about what to actually *do* on stage. The first thing we do in our format is to have an, er, physical reaction to whatever the suggestion inspires us to do.

Inspired by *"rectal itch,"* we walked stiff-legged in

obvious discomfort. We slunk down on chairs and rubbed our backsides against the edges. We squeezed goopy glop into our palms and had trouble with the tubes. Lastly, we exhaled and reached heavenward in relief. During all of this we were in good communication, sharing a world-view which, thankfully, was not physically real.

Most people think that financial systems actually, tangibly, exist outside of the human beings who affect and are affected by them. Sort of like the sets to a Renaissance Faire. Every autumn people dress up in their finest tunics and bustiers to flock to the outdoor shells of 16th century eateries and blacksmythes and lutists. Revelers joust, eat too many whole turkey legs, and swig mead, hopefully in that order. Then they go back to their normal lives. The sets stay put all winter, spring and summer, forlornly awaiting next year's crop of revelers. Financial systems are not like that. When all the people go home, the systems cease to exist. Think Potemkin villages.

Take the movie *It's a Wonderful Life.* Jimmy Stewart plays George Bailey, the son of a small town banker who has inherited the business from his father. He does not love banking, but decides to stay in Bedford Falls and do his duty. Finally he falls in love, and is just leaving on his honeymoon when there is a run on the bank. People fill the building clamoring for their money.

Jimmy/George raises a hand and says, "You're thinking of this place all wrong, as if I have the money back in a safe. Why, your money is in Joe's house, that's right next to yours, and Mrs. Maitland's house, and a hundred others . . . We've got to stick together, we've got to have faith in each other."

Mollified by his charm and generosity (he lends all of his honeymoon money to those who need it to get by), the townspeople disperse, having learned a valuable lesson: this stuff isn't real—and the system only works as long as we believe it will. Just because your neighbor's house sold doesn't mean yours will. Just because stock closed at $100 a share doesn't mean you'll get $100 when you go to sell yours. Just because you get a bank statement doesn't mean you can go there and get your money.

Improv only works because the actors believe it will. We all strive mightily to let fly from a place where we trust ourselves and our scene partners. The currency of trust is all we have to spend, and the sooner we convert trust into faith, the funnier our scenes will be.

Yes, and . . .

This theory is called "Yes, and..." It is based on the idea that in "real" life people are always throwing up barriers to agreement and connectivity. I ask my friend to meet me for lunch and she says "Sorry, I'm out of town." My son asks us to move out for a few days so he can have the house to himself and his friends for his eighteenth birthday. I demur.

In improv, we accept, and build a world where acceptance is normal. My friend rushes back to meet me, arriving bedraggled and half-starved, having driven all night. She stopped on the way at my favorite Italian grocery, threw a brick through the window, donned her superhero cape, and absconded with all my favorite esoteric ingredients for our lunch. I not only grant my son the privilege of being home alone, I stock the place with every available pleasure tool. I fly in celebrities from *Entourage*, hire a photographer for memory shots, and leave a large pile of $100 bills on the mail table for him and his friends. And the car keys. These actions, which demonstrate *over-agreement*, are funny. Our troupe tries to present real life - the way it should be - on the stage. No argument that in real life we should all be seeing a lot more agreement!

Investment decisions, being ephemeral, are also based on agreement. We all agree with key concepts, like the business cycle (values go up, then down, then up), market values, and profit = good. These shared beliefs are what keeps the financial system in place.

Our financial system is also based on connectivity, both figuratively and literally. In Tom Clancy's *Debt of Honor*, the bad guys insert a programming glitch into the operations of the US stock market. It only lasts a few minutes, but causes an economic meltdown of enormous proportions.

I once participated in a sales pitch to information technology decision-makers at Federated Department Stores. Federated, owners of Bloomingdales and Macy's, told us that when the telephone connection between the registers and the credit card authorizers went down, floor supervisors were authorized to swipe credit cards through the machine for future processing and then let customers walk off with the merchandise. They told us that this caused them to lose $1 million dollars *an hour* in uncollectible debts. This horrifying fact showed me how clearly financial systems are castles in the air, ephemeral "networks of trust" which don't really exist in the corporeal world.

Power of Three

In improv we rely heavily on the power of three. One popular format, called *the Harold*, sets out three story lines, then develops each of them in three parts each, called beats. The first beat lays out the relationship, theme, and dramatic tension. The second beat cements these elements. The third beat (for which our troupe is named) resolves conflicts, and, ideally, interweaves elements of all three story lines together.

Finance calls the power of three "diversification."

Your portfolio should contain stocks, bonds, and cash – though not necessarily in that order. There are many subvariations within these three categories and it almost doesn't matter which ones you choose as long as you spread the money around. This is because nobody knows what will happen to your money, now, or (frankly) ever. This is not a bad thing. We do not want the secrets found out. If there were no elements of risk or luck, and random weirdness, we would all keep the money under the mattress because no one would speculate and thus there would be no market. Where's the fun in that?

Stocks represent fractional ownership of a company that wants to be owned by the public at large. When a company decides to ask the public for money (I call this "begging") they offer up a piece of themselves in return for cash. People buy stock because they hope that their little piece will eventually be worth more than they paid for it, so they can cash out at a profit. They also hope that the company to whom they have given their hard-earned cash will reward them by giving some of it back in dividends. Many stockholders wish that the dividend rate and perhaps even the frequency with which they get paid will increase. (I only ask that you note the use of the words "hope" and "wish" in this paragraph!)

Once the company is public, the stockholders are always jockeying for position - buying, selling, buying again. The vast majority of stock owners give their money not to the issuing company but to somebody who bought it from somebody who bought it from somebody who invested it originally. This, by the way, is called the "secondary market."

Bonds are just a fancy way of saying "debt." When you buy bonds, you essentially lend money, as opposed to stocks, when you just give it away and hope to get it back. Stocks can go wildly up, wildly down - or anywhere in between. Bonds are also traded based on guesstimates of whether or not the borrowing corporation or public entity (e.g., the State of Oregon) is deemed more or less likely to pay you back. Again, no one knows what will happen, no one will ever know, and "past performance is no guarantee of future results."

Cash is not just what you have in your savings account,

it is also "cash-like" investments such as Certificates of Deposit (CDs) and Treasury Bills. With Certificates of Deposit you give your cash to a bank and tell them you won't ask for it back for a defined period, say three months to five years. During this time the bank takes your money and lends it to someone else who pays them interest. Banks hope the interest rate they get is higher than the interest rate they commit to pay to little you. With Treasury Bills you lend money to the government, who commits to use their "full faith and credit" (note use of the word "faith") to pay you back. Treasury Bills are supposed to be "risk free." I personally would believe that the US will pay me back but not necessarily the Government of Rwanda.

Group Mind

In improv, you are the playwright, director, actor, and costume designer. The only sounds and props that exist are those which you create and make the audience believe in. Just to make it harder, everyone else on stage with you also plays these roles. If you're lucky, magic happens. We call it "group mind." This is when scene partners are deeply listening and emotionally, physically, and intellectually responsive.

There are lots of ways to build group mind. One is called *Twenty-One.* A group stands in a circle, shoulders touching, eyes closed. One person says "one," another "two," etc. Whenever two people speak at once we start over. It can take two minutes or forever to get to twenty-one but the experience is excellent practice as it forces us to deeply listen to each other, anticipate who will do what, and find our own place in the game.

At one improv festival, Third Beat decided to do a series of café scenes, essentially pairs sitting at makeshift tables having conversations. We wanted the conversations to be hyper-real. We had three groups of two, and one loner. We were not in one another's sight lines but the acoustics were good and we could hear. Our goal was to all talk at once, taking turns being audible. Again, our word was "*grenade*." One story was about dropping a conversational "bomb" that never went off. Another demonstrated an explosive situation between two people, and a third was two women wondering why men like to watch war movies when you could get enough violent explosions in a house full of teenagers. The person who was alone became a loudly irascible veteran who began his rant with, "I was there. I saw the bombs go off. I sensed the shrapnel."

Throughout our fifteen minutes we pretty successfully passed key phrases around from conversation to conversation, essentially operating four split-screens simultaneously. But we had entirely forgotten to plan how to end our show! Here's where the group mind just worked...the way it is supposed to. One by one, the couples took their conversations to organic ending points and walked off the stage holding hands. We did this, mind you, without ever actually looking at one another, and it was a beautiful, completely unplanned ending to our show.

Finance tries to have "group mind" in the form of an

efficient market with access to perfect information (Keynes' Doctrine), but I've mostly experienced the sensation through herd mentality. The Director of Investor Relations at MCI, during a time when their stock was going up faster than any other stock in the world (even corrected for currency valuations), once spoke to a class I was teaching. He said that "the market runs on fear, hope, and greed." How can things be fine September 10, 2001 and completely wretched September 11? Answer: they're not. Markets are never fine, or wretched. They are a living, breathing, ephemeral representation of group mind.

Want vs. Need

Improvisers are funny because they are hyper-real. Nobody wants to pay money to see people being boring. But we can't be fake, or try to be funny. Instead, our goal is to present highly concentrated versions of recognizable human situations. We do this by making our objectives important, and call this concept "want vs. need." When we want something we can express our longings on a continuum from preference to pathological. Preferences aren't particularly interesting. If I prefer coffee but will take tea I am not passionate about my choice and the audience won't care much either way. Put another way, if we don't really care the audience won't either. A need, on the other hand, is stark. It can be life or death. A scene where I am likely to die if I don't get my coffee is pretty funny. The obituary could read "Out of Sumatran."

Good improvisers are able to communicate quickly what they need and their point of view about not having it to their scene partners. Bad scenes usually go something like this:

"Hey, Joe."
"Hey."
"How ya doin'?"
"Fine. You?"

Good scenes look something like this:

"Marco! Get this safe off my back!"

Immediately we arrive in the middle of the story, smack-dab into a dramatic conflict. Will Marco come? Or will the poor bank robber get left behind while his compadre absconds with the loot and the sirens get louder in the background? *We care.*

Financial decisions force clarification of wants vs. needs because they demand tradeoffs. If I want $10,000 a month after taxes that's nice for me but unless I am willing to dramatically change my lifestyle I am not likely to get it. Praying for miracles won't help. If I need money for a bone marrow transplant I am suddenly very able to make the necessary sacrifices to come up with it. In my experience it is much better to make financial decisions that address needs vs. wants. Contrary to popular opinion (I read a headline today that three out of five baby boomers do not have enough saved for retirement), much of us are over-saved for wants. I think we only need to save for needs.

Here is why: our conception of retirement, health,

lifespan, education, and family are all up for grabs. You or I could go at any time. We need to be using our money to get what we want, in the only now we have! If we have people we can trust and believe in, and they have us, there will be enough money to get what we need.

It is all very scary. We could lose everything, sell our souls along the way, and have a truly terrible performing experience. I don't care whether you embrace the fear, or try to use it with gritted teeth. Just follow where it leads. In finance, as well as in improv, it's the only way to be successful.

Chapter One

How to Win Money Fights With Your Significant Other

It all started with a chair. I wanted purple, a big eggplant scoop of a thing. Cozy, obvious, made for two. Overstuffed, in more than one sense of the word. It cost $250. My husband wanted a little brown rotating disk. Low to the ground and as understated as it was possible to be while still inhabiting the physical realm. Reserved. Boring. Anal. Cost: $1,200. He said my chair was low-class and tacky. His chair-ish object was so nondescript it bordered on the pompous, a fact I unwisely chose to comment on. We had been married for years and never had this "discussion" before. We walked out of the store empty-handed (and yes, that's an unfortunate pun).

The bedrock concept in improvisational comedy is agreement. When you improvise you are the playwright, director, actor, sound person, and prop master. And so are your scene partners. If we behaved on stage the way we behave in life, disagreeing and looking out for Number One, every scene would be chaos. Nobody would pay to see self-centered posturing; we can get that every day. But if the improvisers are able to create a world where everyone agrees to play together, magic happens. This concept is called "Yes, and . . ."

Imagine a scene like this:

> "Pull over, Ma'am. The speed limit is thirty-five in a work zone."
> "Sorry, officer. I am late to a Weight Watchers meeting."
> "And I see your license is expired."
> "Oh my God, I am terribly, terribly ashamed."

"And it lists your weight at one-twenty-five."
(Holding trigger finger to own temple) "May I borrow your gun?"

This scene is funny because the speeding driver agrees with the arresting officer that she is not only a lawbreaker but a despicable human being who is fat and therefore does not deserve to live. What if the scene went something like this:

"Pull over, Ma'am. The speed limit is thirty-five in a work zone."
"But I was only going thirty."
"My radar says otherwise."
"But I was only going thirty."

This scene died the minute the speeder argued with the officer's opening remarks. The characters did not agree to be in the same world, instead the scene became a negotiation over who was right. Not funny.

Agreement is also the bedrock concept in winning a money fight with someone you care about, with whom you will likely want to live to fight again.

To get agreement with someone else you must first establish agreement with yourself. Call it congruity, internal consistency, making your outside (your spending and not-spending choices) match your inside (your values, background, biases). You are what you spend. Find your definition of "good," and work it for dear life. You are the playwright, director, actor, sound person, and prop master.

Your significant other also plays all of these roles, with his own definition of "good." Hopefully, there will be an overlap, and you will find a middle ground. My husband and I eventually *agreed* on a pair of mid-size, mid-price, plush light gray chairs, which swiveled like the brown one. They lasted longer than the marriage did.

We eventually made a furniture store happy because we found a shared perspective on what the chairs represented to us at that particular point in our lives together.

Gloria Steinem said, "If you want to know what your priorities are, look in your checkbook." What is the point of the money in our checkbooks? If we are all, to some degree, spending a large part of our life trying to get it - and more of our life deciding whether or how to spend it - we ought to know when to declare victory! We ought to know our own definitions of "good."

For me, it wasn't about the chair, it was what the chair made me imagine. I saw cuddly togetherness, sharing a newspaper, sunshine streaming in the window making the fabric glow. Maybe a child in my blissfully married arms. He saw himself embarrassed, blocking the view of the offending item whenever friends came over, saying, "She picked that, against my better judgment," and "I wanted the modern one. In taupe."

In the end, it wasn't about the chair, or even about the money, but what the purchase represented, the story behind the money. Every single purchase or non-purchase means something and contributes to individuals' own stories. Added up, the sum of these millions of decisions are as unique as a fingerprint. As Freud said, there are no accidents. Financial decisions are made along three different storylines:

Pure survival, and its cousin, basic functionality, i.e., somewhere to sit down.

Status/Fun/Pleasure. You know what this is, I hope.

Helping others. Beware. This can be good or bad.

Most financial decisions have elements of all three, so choose a decision you've recently made, and perform the following highly scientific self-assessment to find your own storyline or "filter." Choose a financial activity, then assess how many behaviors fit into each category:

Five Signs of A Survivalist

1. You have savings automatically deducted from your bank account.
2. You balance your checkbook within two hours of receiving the statement.
3. You drive ten miles out of your way to get cheaper gas, even with a screaming child in a car-seat.
4. You spend more time finding the cheapest air-fare/hotel combinations than the total hours you will be away on the vacation you're shopping for.
5. You believe there is no such thing as "old" clothes.

Five Signs of a Status Seeker

1. You wear excellent shoes (this is always always the tipoff).
2. You can look down right now and see at least one designer label. On the outside of the garment.
3. You always look extra good in airports.
4. You do not take the bus, even when it is the most convenient mode of transportation.
5. You are a humongous tipper, but only when dining with others.

Five Signs of A Helper

1. You donate money to everyone who asks. Even telemarketers and drunks.
2. You let others eat off your plate.
3. You stack your dishes at a restaurant to make life easier for the server.
4. You always have change.
5. You are a humongous tipper, even when dining alone.

You will be more likely to win financial arguments if you know your own definition of "good." Once you figure out yours and stick to it with a calm, internally consistent point of view, you are more likely to get what you want. The person whose inside most closely matches their outside always attracts the resources. The best story wins.

The trick is understanding how to quantify "good."

There are four different ways to define "good" in a

financial sense: asset utilization, revenue, profit, and cash flow. Think of them as four friends who dropped by for dinner, all with their own particular culinary preferences. One likes fish, another hates it, the third is allergic to nuts and the fourth will only eat food that is white (really). Each one wants to eat a delicious meal through the filter of their own particular point of view. And you, as the cook/host, have a limited amount of time and money with which to feed your guests. You must make trade-offs to find the definition of "good" which keeps the greatest number of guests well away from the epi-pen.

Asset Utilization is "shopping in your closet." Assets are things that you own, whether or not they are fully paid for yet. "Asset" does not mean "good." The broken stereo is an asset, so are the size four pink jeans I will never wear again. Assets last more than a year, and wear out over time. Good asset utilizers keep assets going longer than they are supposed to last, do not buy more than they need, do not waste money keeping dead assets on life-support, and are brave enough to invest when they see a good deal. Jerry Seinfeld with his forty-six Porsches is a bad asset utilizer. So is the person who never cleans out his garage. So is the person who waits until the car is completely broken before trading it in. So is the investor who is too scared to take risks and misses the next Microsoft, because, sometimes, assets appreciate.

To find the stories which best show asset utilization, use one or more of the following theories: "The Russian," total cost of ownership, opportunity cost and "The Greater Fool."

"The Russian" is my favorite. Since goods under communism were traditionally hard to find, when you saw something that was never coming again you grabbed it regardless of the cost. I once walked into a store in Florence, lured by the amethyst dress in the window (apparently I have a thing for purple), pulled out my credit card, closed my eyes, and signed. To this day I have no idea what that dress cost. It epitomized the trip for me whenever I wore it and I wore it until it disintegrated.

Speaking of disintegration, I was thrilled to find a celery green linen suit at Alcott and Andrews in San Francisco when I was there on a business trip. It was unusually inexpensive and I snapped it up. Soon after I wore it to a business meeting, where I had the temerity to lean too far over the drinking fountain, causing water to splash on my lapel. The water made a spot. Not realizing what had caused the mark, I daubed at the affected area with some seltzer water. Which made a bigger spot. Big dry cleaning bill ensued. My relationship with the suit went something like this: Spot. Bill. Spot. Bill. Every time I wanted to wear the suit I had to check the weather, foreswear all food and drink, and ensure the air was cooled to a non-sweat-inducing temperature. Given that this was practically never, the "bargain" suit turned out to be exorbitantly priced, and I eventually gave it away. The sticker price was a great deal, the total cost of ownership was not! Total cost of ownership is another way to evaluate asset utilization. It's not the car but the cost of driving the car. Not the toy but the cost of the toy + batteries. Not the razor but the razor *with* the blades.

"On Sale": words that turn logic to mush. Just because an item is on sale doesn't mean it's a good deal. Buying on sale *never* saves a penny. The money still mysteriously leaves your pocket. Worst, we buy something that is just okay and doesn't really fit the bill. The question in the back of your mind should be, "If this item were full price would I be buying it ?" Unless the item is being purchased for survival/functionality, just...walk...away. If you can't do that, then at least keep the tag on and hold on to the receipt.

Okay, you say, I could walk away. I don't desperately need it, but it will make me happy. Retail therapy is alive and well. But will you still love it tomorrow? The item you lust for may be cheaper than a visit to a shrink, less fattening than a package of donuts, and more eco-friendly than speeding with the top down. But the true price of every purchase extends beyond what's on the tag – the true price is the cost of buying one thing and not another. This concept is called "opportunity cost." There is a cost of you spending your time reading these words versus sweeping the floor, taking a bath, or feeding the hungry. Every item you buy takes up space in your psyche as well as in your house. The more stuff you have on the outside that doesn't "match" your inside, the weaker your financial power becomes.

I am reminded of a seminal scene from the television show *Sex in the City*. Carrie Bradshaw has decided to buy her apartment. She is bemoaning the fact that she has no savings. Then she realizes that she has many many pairs of Manolo Blahniks, at roughly $700 a pair. She does the math and is shocked to discover that she would have the downpayment by now if she had not succumbed to The Power of The Shoe.

Carrie would have been okay if there was a strong market for used Blahniks (check eBay – I found "Manolo Blahniks from Sex in the City" starting at $300) but I doubt she'd get more than she paid. Assets appreciate when future buyers line up to snag them. Nobody knows what makes this happen exactly, no one will ever know, and we do not ever want to find out. If there was a secret, and it was revealed, nobody would ever speculate and the concept of "market" would be over.

Assets appreciate when people are willing to take a risk and speculate. They only speculate when they think another speculator will come behind them who is willing to pay more than they did and cash them out. The second speculator only comes if he thinks there is a third speculator waiting in the wings, etc. etc. etc. This is literally called "The Greater Fool Theory."

Assets also appreciate when there are more buyers than sellers, or somebody thinks there will be more buyers than sellers at a later date. When my youngest son was little he loved Beanie Babies and was continually valuing and re-valuing his collection, then using the (hypothetical) inflated value to lobby for the latest "Halloweenie Beanie" (not kidding).

Revenue is how you define a sale. If you have a job, your salary is your revenue, because you sold your time. If you are a citizen of the US you pay revenue to the government in the form of taxes collected by the Internal *Revenue* Service. When you purchase something at a store, you generate revenue for the owners. When you buy a college education, at least part of the point of the experience is to help you get a job which generates revenue.

Revenue can be good or bad, depending on what you have to do to get it, and whether or not it can be sustained. More isn't necessarily better; neither is less. At the same time, and in the short term, we cannot necessarily control the amount of salary we are able to earn. But we can decide whether or not our current revenue position meets our definition of "good." We can decide whether or not to try to do something about it in the medium to long term.

Interestingly, revenue is not always actual, factual money and hence is not the same as cash. Companies use the term to reflect their best guess formula about how much they sold. But "sold" does not always equal "collected."

Profit is the difference between revenue and expenses. If your college education cost $60,000 and you earn $30,000, you are not profitable short-term, unless you move back in with your parents, and even then it will take two to three years to break even, after taxes. Like revenue, profit can be good or bad, depending upon where it comes from and whether it can be sustained. Put another way, getting rich quick is usually a bad idea, getting rich slowly can definitely work.

Being profitable is good because it brings a sense of

security and money is available for a rainy day. Profitability is also the foundational tenet of a capitalistic society which exists to deliver profits to owners. Profitability can be bad because it can force drastic expense cuts which end up costing more in the long run, like not going to the dentist every six months or not fixing the leak in the roof. Profitability can also be bad because it obviates necessary investments, which can close the door to innovation, efficiencies of scale, and social progress (see Chapter Seven, "Should You Give a Mouse a Cookie?").

Because the profit calculation starts with revenue, which is not tangible, profit is not tangible either. When your tax return shows a profit of $50,000 you don't necessarily (ha!) have $50,000 in your checking account.

Cash flow, on the other hand, is always real and always good. It happens when money comes in faster than it goes out. As Wimpy said, "I will gladly pay you Tuesday for a hamburger today." Many vendors give a 2% discount if the bill is paid in full in thirty days or less. When people don't have cash to live on, they tend to whip out their credit cards, producing cash flow now but increasing debt.

The point of debt is to borrow money you don't have now, buy an asset, and then repay the debt. If you're using debt to eat, there is no asset involved. If you're using debt to buy an asset that doesn't appreciate, that's not a great position to be in from a profitability standpoint, even though debt does enable the cash to flow.

So now that you know that asset utilization, revenue, profit, and cash flow are the four distinct ways to define "good," and have a sense of your personal filters, it's time to win the argument. Quantify your definition of "good," then quantify your opponent's. Here is a set of sample arguments:

> Okay: "This purple chair will last a long time and make me happy."
>
> Better: "This purple chair will last ten years, costing us only twenty-five dollars a year. It is easy to sponge off so we won't need professional cleaning, and it will make me happy."
>
> Even better (if it were true): "This purple chair will last ten years, costing us only twenty-five dollars a year. Because it goes with everything we have we don't need to buy a new rug or coffee table or lamp (total cost fifteen hundred dollars). And it will make me happy."
>
> Winning (but completely not true): "If we don't like it, we can sell it for more than we paid."

...and that's why I didn't get my eggplant-colored chair!

You may have noticed a lot of language about making me happy. This is known as a "soft" benefit. There are soft and hard benefits and costs. Soft benefits and costs are emotional and, as such, subjective. Hard costs are when there is a bill to be paid, hard benefits are when the money coming in is bigger and faster than the money going out. While hard costs are painful and real, soft costs also hurt. Hard benefits are real, but soft benefits can feel even more tangible.

So, we are back full circle to the point of the asset (chair): to give me pleasure. Please note that if I hadn't quantified the benefits using one of the super-duper asset utilization tricks, and merely said, in a pathetic voice, "You don't want to make me happy?" I would have lost the argument because it is an inherently weak position. What is happiness? Why, out of all the chairs in the world, am I wedded to this particular chair? What kind of a person can only be happy with a hunk of eggplant-colored plush glowing warmly in a ray of sunshine with a cup of great coffee, a loved one, and the *New York Times* in hand? If I get the chair I want, will I be happy once and for all, or soon will we be fighting over a fabulous pumpkin-colored ottoman?

Winning financial arguments is based on making your inside match your outside, the best definition of "good." Like improvisational comedy, the best scenes are based on agreement about the world you inhabit together. Throw in a little knowledge about asset utilization, revenue, profit, and cash flow, and you up the odds of not only winning the argument but securing a pleasurable financial future.

Chapter Two

Send My Spinach to China

Who hasn't seen an exasperated parent admonish their vegetable-spurning children to be grateful because people are starving in China? Granted that was before China became a superpower, but you get the idea.

I think it is good to waste resources, money included, and that everybody should do it more. Don't get me wrong – I can be as frugal as the next person. When I was a little girl, I liked to get my allowance in quarters, which I would then stack in a corner of my closet. I enjoyed just holding them in my hand. The heft, the shape, the shininess all promised a future world of money under my control. When I was in college I pilfered toilet paper from the movie theater on campus and made my own soap and shampoo. Ask me about the myriad uses for apple cider vinegar….

I've also been to Mumbai and seen hundreds of children living in pipes. And to Soweto.

Still, my advice is to waste money regularly. Just plan it in advance. All of you dieters out there know that most people end up heavier after the diet is over than before it started. This is because we, I mean "they," starve ourselves until the scale becomes our friend, then go back to normal. To get down to 114 once I joined Weight Watchers and subsisted on little else but whiting. Google it… and you'll see just how awful that decision turned out to be!

Then I read some great weight-loss advice: eat one terrific dessert a week. Lemon meringue pie. Sticky toffee pudding. Hot and gooey Thai coconut custard. My teeth are aching just writing this. But the secret is, you eat just one. And you plan it, look forward to it, go hog wild - then stop.

Same thing should go for money. Plan a weekly splurge for, say, twenty-five to fifty dollars. The rest of the time bring your lunch, refill the water bottle, and settle for the break room coffee. But plan your "cheat."

Much of my work these past few years has been in London, which contains Harrods. Harrods is nothing less than a shopper's paradise. Advertised on its web-page as "the world's most famous luxury store," it was owned until 2010 by Mohamed Al-Fayed, father of Dodi who was the boyfriend of Princess Di. There are statues of both of them at Harrods, and soon Michael Jackson will come too. Wikipedia notes, "In 2007, Harrods hired a live Egyptian cobra to protect the shoe counter, guarding a £62,000 ($84,880) pair of haute couture ruby-, sapphire- and diamond-encrusted sandals launched by designer Rene Caovilla." But I digress.

My strategy with Harrods was to walk confidently right by the battalions of exquisitely dressed sales-people/shoplifting police, breathe in the heady mix of perfumed air, and enthusiastically buy the fanciest...hair clip...they had. It cost $35. But I splurged and found a way to enjoy the full Harrods experience. This, dear reader, is what I am recommending to you. Denying oneself is a bitch and always backfires eventually. Plus, you could be dead tomorrow.

When people think about wasting money they focus on the common tendency to buy too much stuff. I think there are two other ways to waste it: hold on too long to what we do not need; and forego taking risks out of fear they will go bad.

I can only point to the TV show *Hoarders* to illustrate the economic cost of holding on to possessions for dear life. People get crushed by their stuff!

Stacy and Clinton of *What Not to Wear* always make their subjects throw out most of what they own as a way to make way to start over. The clothes that make people look like everything from pole dancers to Amish milkmaids are taking up psychic space and weighing them down. When Stacy and Clinton counsel people on making purchases that better reflect the best things about them (the show gives each subject $5,000 to finance these acquisitions), they talk in terms of "cost per wearing," not sticker price. Things you own and do not wear end up being very very expensive. Feng shui proponents will tell you that every object represents positive or negative life force. I'm no expert, but surely the search for good "*qi*" can't include not being able to open the junk drawer. Net net, holding onto stuff too long costs you, and not just in money but in psychic well-being.

Junk hauling, by the way, is big business. One purveyor, "College Hunks Hauling Junk," actually expanded during the recent recession. Just sayin'.

Recycling is also booming. Interestingly, unless you're talking about aluminum cans, recycling is a waste of money and energy. It actually costs more to haul, sort, and process recycled waste than to dump it in a landfill. Recycling makes us pay attention and feel good, and that in itself may well be worth the roughly $8 billion we spend doing it.

As it turns out, "the desire to use natural resources encourages people to conserve them and even, to the extent possible, create more of them," as Daniel K. Benjamin points out in *Eight Great Myths of Recycling*. I believe the same thing is true about money. Human beings are unbelievably creative at problem-solving when we want to be. The effort to conserve resources, done well, can actually cause us to be smarter about generating them in the first place. But only if we waste a few along the way. Even in bankruptcy there is a "normal" entertainment budget of $100 a month. *USA Today* recently reported that Americans in debt worry about money an average of 3.3 hours per day. Talk about a waste!

But wasting a little money on purpose can:

- Be really really fun. See you at Harrods!
- Keep you from wasting more when you go off the diet.
- Make you more grateful for what you have.
- Help you attract resources from others because you are grateful and happy.

Conversely, holding on to every penny for dear life can also cost us money. In my experience, the biggest mistake most people make in investing isn't failing to take a risk, but in failing to cash out when that risk goes south. Cutting our losses is just hard for us humans to do. My theory is that we somehow feel guilty for having made the purchase in the first place, so admitting it was a mistake becomes too humiliating to face. So we hide, and just pray for our investment to get back to what we bought it for so we can sell it.

Avoiding risks is also wasting resources, because a mind-set of scarcity is too often engendered by fear. In my work with numerous non-profits and small businesses as well as with corporate departments faced with budgeting, the most common mistake isn't spending too much money. It is spending too little, letting great opportunities pass by. This happens because, as those of us with control needs know all too well, not spending money gives us a sense of control, while taking risks does the opposite.

Improvisational comedy is based on the concept that risks are not only good, but essential to finding the funny. The whole goal is to free us up from all of our filters and let whatever happens happen. We practice this with the "Five Things" exercise. One person points to another and says, "Five Things You Don't Want Your Mother to Know About You," or "Five Hypothetical Tropical Diseases," or "Five Names for an Emo Band." You get the idea, just run your mouth without trying to make sense of what comes out.

I won't deny that it's a terrifying feeling to take the stage with nothing and just see what happens. It is terribly tempting to plan an entrance, be it with a physicality, a great line, or a pre-conceived relationship, but this nearly always backfires. We try to make the reality of the scene fit our plan, and that is disrespectful to our scene partners and our audience. Many stand-up comedians fail at improv for just this reason: they are essentially looking for opportunities to do their schtick. A schtick is just scene-stealing by another name.

One of the best improv tools I've ever used takes our planning tendency and turns it on its head. It is called "Blind Initiations." Each person turns his or her back and quickly plans to start a scene, completely independently, and "blind" to what their scene partner is doing. They enter and deliver opening lines which rarely have anything whatsoever to do with one another, but, as the scene develops and people listen, beautiful castles get built.

One guy comes out as a stealthy soldier in the jungle, knees bent, cradling a rifle. He turns sharply, yet silently, careful not to rustle the undergrowth. The other guy walks out standing fully erect. He is clumsy, turning in small circles with a half-open mouth, and confusedly remarks, "I doooon't think we should have left the circus." This scene, despite (or perhaps because of) the risks taken, ended up being very funny.

Maybe I have now expanded your definition of "waste," and you're thinking about taking my advice and blowing some money for fun, tossing all the crap you don't need, and carpe diem-ing once in a while. How do you know when you are successful?

When people ask me questions like, "How much do I

need to save to become financially secure?" or "How do I pay for college?" I always respond by asking them to define "good." They say, "I want to make money," and eye me suspiciously like, "huh?" Unless they know in advance what their evaluative criteria are (one of the few things I actually learned in graduate school), they are in no position to know when to bail.

So I advise them to write their definition of "good" on a piece of paper and stick it in a drawer. The definition has to have numbers and a time frame. "Make money" is not good enough, for if they made half a percent in ten years they wouldn't be boasting. In essence, the decision to invest has to have a bookended decision to un-invest. And both need a purpose at the get-go.

Once a respected friend and former colleague asked me if I wanted to become a "founding investor" of his startup long distance company. This was in the nineties, when people still bought long distance separately from local service. And they still had phones in their houses. I was working with a lot of companies that sold long distance, liked the guy, and figured it was now or never to put my money where my mouth was. I asked George, what's the least I can invest? He said, ten thousand. Long pause. George, I said, it's my kid's college education. He said, trust me. I ended up with a lovely plexiglass pyramid celebrating my founding investor status. For three entire years. Then the company went public. As soon as I could I took out my initial $10,000. The stock went on to grow nicely, and I ended up making three times what I originally put in.

That was my definition of "good," to get my $10,000 back. But it scared the pants off me and I never did it again. Yet I learned how to define "good."

In the improv world it's terribly hard to define "good," and a lot of people's feelings get hurt along the way. But we have to try.

Start by questioning the adage "Waste not, want not." If you need resources you'll find a way to create them, and hanging onto old baggage will not, I repeat will *not* help!

Chapter Three

Is Having Kids a Good Financial Move? Performing Improv?

The definitive answer is easy: No.

You don't need to read any further. The average middle-income family will spend $222,360 to raise a baby born in 2009. This does not include college, which can multiply the number by one and a half to two.

That's just for children who are living with their birth families. It doesn't include the cost of adoption (up to $40,000, less any tax credits) to get the rug rat in the house in the first place. And that's just for one adoption try! If medical means are necessary to conceive that also obviously ups the price; in vitro fertilization costs about $11,000 per cycle, and it "normally" (word used advisedly) takes three cycles, but some people have nine!

So a nearly-quarter-million-dollar hit is on the low end! It doesn't include lost wages in case one or both parties takes unpaid time off from work. Or the quantification of productivity loss from extreme sleep deprivation. Once a very accomplished friend of mine was driving shortly after she had her first child. She stopped at a light, then actually *forgot how to use the stick!*

Those are the financial minuses. What are the plusses? In the most macabre of senses, your child is only worth $220,000. And that's if chopped into bits to sell for parts.

Bone marrow fetches the most coin. Organs used to be hot, but now they're not. Someday the kid's DNA might be worth something, though. The good news is that it's exportable without harm, so you can always hope to at least break even!

Other than the cultural, biological, and sentimental reasons for childbirth, not covered here, having kids is a bad financial move if you live in a developed country.

Children used to be financially necessary. Unless the mother died in childbirth (which she had a 40% chance of doing in the 1800s), people had a lot of children because they were needed to work on the farm. In the 1800s, the average US woman had *seven* children, and died at 40 (a Catch 22 if I ever heard one!). As urbanization replaced frontier living, birth rates fell and life expectancy rose, though not necessarily in that order. Now the birthrate is 1.83 children per family.

Poor people still have more children than non-poor. There is a reason that China's economy is booming (though that in itself does not mean all is well!) due to the one-child family. Overpopulation is considered by many to severely threaten resources. I ask you only one thing: what do we do to deer when Bambi eats the backyard corn crop?

Assuming we don't shoot them, now that most children aren't working the farm, what (financial) good are they? According to the economic theory of fertility, children are treated, it's been said, like commodities in an economic equation.

In Nigeria, kids can become street hawkers, especially

of pre-paid calling cards and mobile phones. If you have your own business, they can have real jobs and get tax-deductible wages. They can even run the business after you die, though fewer than a third decide to take over and that doesn't always work out.

Of course, there is always modeling, acting, or becoming a professional athlete while still a minor, though only a fraction of kids are good enough.

Okay, so we could put the kids to work. Aside from that, what financial good are they? I used to say I had ten children in the bodies of two. My two young men (who will always be my babies) were born when I was thirty-five and thirty-eight, purposely well after my business rep was established. Despite creating the embarrassing need to pump breast milk on airplanes, my sons actually increased my earnings potential dramatically in two key ways.

First, I learned to work in my head, because the tiny moments I had two hands free to sit at my computer were virtually nonexistent. Especially the two hands free part. We tried to live the theory that children need touch more than anything else. We actually *wore* our kids 24x7, family bed and all. Their little tootsies never touched the ground until they clambered out of the Snugli and took their first halting steps. My singular life goal from about 1989 until 1995 was to wear earrings. This required the aforementioned two hands, sufficient brain function to make a choice, and enough sleep to achieve small motor control. There were many days when none of these criteria was met. Not even close.

But working in my head had some advantages. I mentally slow-cooked my deliverables, so that when my fingers were free to touch the keys the words just flowed.

Having children also helped me prioritize, so lots of scut work simply went undone. Along with picking up the toy room, going to the grocery store, and the button-front waistbands on my pants.

While there are some plusses, the net calculation is that having children is a financal disaster. So hey – you could just plain sell them. When the US had slavery, children were slaves if their mothers were slaves. Before Lincoln signed the Emancipation Proclamation he considered remuneration to slave owners for relieving them of their "property." Children weren't worth a whole lot, but every little bit helped.

Assuming you find this argument distasteful and decide not to sell your child, after you've spent a quarter to a half *million* dollars per, will they at least take care of you if you're old and broke?

Here there may actually be some good news. According to the US Census Bureau, the number of parents who moved into their adult children's houses increased 67% from 2.1M in 2000 to 3.6M in 2007. Average adults in this situation pay 10% of their income to support their parents. So if your kid ends up rich, and you live a very long time, you may come out ahead, even accounting for the *time value of money*.

The concept of time value of money helps us see the

present impact of future financial activities. Money comes in, money goes out - but we want it to come in early and go out late, not the other way around.

Wimpy said, "I will gladly pay you Tuesday for a hamburger today." All of us want to buy now, pay later. The time value of money idea helps us decide how much we need to get now to make paying later a good idea. It's a simple concept which, like many financial precepts, sounds like a smarty-pants show-off. (For example, the time value of money is also called "discounted cash flow." I ask you, who wants their cash flow to be discounted?)

If you put $100 in a savings account at 10% interest, after a year you have $110. After two years you have $121 ($110 x 1.10, because you still have the original $110, which is represented by the 1, plus 10%, which is .10 = $110). After three years you have $133.10 in your hot little hands. And you are also living in some kind of alternative universe because nowhere on earth can you (legally) get a bank to pay you 10% interest. Nevertheless, the time value of money looks at this scenario from the opposite end of a telescope. It answers the question, "How much do I have to get in the future to cover what I've spent today?"

No matter how much money most comedic improvisers get in the future, it oh-so-rarely covers what we are spending on our craft today.

Like child-raising, improv is also a terrible financial choice. And we're not even talking about the cost of countless cartons of Kleenex being crumpled by frightened parents who feel their children are Wasting Their Lives Chasing a Dream.

Unlike film actors whose work is reproduce-able, most stage actors barely get paid. And, sadly, the improv experience rarely if ever translates to the silver screen, or even the small one. (Those amazing guys on *Whose Line Is It Anyway* are freaks of nature.)

Speaking of income, only 2% of Screen Actors Guild members can support themselves from their work. More than half of comedians can't live from comedy alone (can you spell *DAY JOB*?). The best improv gigs (outside of those Shangri la-like Hollywood gigs) are on cruise ships, which pay $2,500 a week, plus room and board. The room in question might just list a little from time to time but hey, it's free. The board could be re-spelled "bored" as actors could be stuck asea for three months at a time, but the job still produces actual funding.

Financial disaster notwithstanding, though, there are things that improv can do that nothing else can. It creates that evanescent moment where life, real, pulsing, completely unpredictable *life*, is staring you in the face. (Come to think of it, that's also probably a big reason why people have children.)

The special never-before-experienced value of impov (corporate types call this "competitive distinctiveness") is that the entire show is *all made up*. As the Zen Master improvisers T.J. and Dave demonstrate in their aptly titled film *Trust Us, This Is All Made Up*, this doesn't mean we don't prepare. We try to maintain a fairly high level of physical fitness and flexibility, as this puts us in touch with our bodies. We walk around all day studying Our Fellow Man. I personally imitate just about everybody I see, hoping they don't notice and clock me.

Good improvisers strive mightily to have a high "reference" level, which is code for knowing a lot about a lot of things. We try to be curious, intrepid, and perhaps a tad wild in our own probably weird ways. The typical improviser was a lonely geek in school (to this day there are an extraordinary number of IT professionals in our ranks) and basically feels like a head on a stick. Still, we prepare and prepare and prepare. My troupe practices once a week, and spends time outside of class structuring our performance format. And then changing it. And changing it again. Theater school costs big bucks - the Yale School of Drama rings in at $27,800, although most students get financial aid. I've personally spent thousands of dollars on classes.

So, if having a child and performing improvisational comedy are such terrible financial choices, why does anybody make them?

Because they are choices that make the rest of your financial life go better.

Also, people aren't rational in any way that economists can define, at least not yet, despite the amazingly accurate technology behind my Netflix recommendations... Improvisational comedy requires such a huge range of skills, talents, commitment, and creativity that it should be, in my humble opinion, one of the top-paid professions, right up there after nurses and teachers. Maybe someday that wish will come true.

Lets pretend for a minute that improvisers do get paid more than, say, the typical outbound call-center representative bothering you at dinnertime. Further, let's imagine that your family becomes, with the addition of progeny, healthier, happier, and generally more photogenic. If these things come to be, will your financial standing improve?

Finance, surprisingly, would say yes, and start talking about the concept of "good will." According to *Investopedia*, "Good will is seen as an *intangible* asset on the balance sheet because it is not a physical asset such as buildings and equipment."

Every company and every person owns stuff. They buy it using money they have saved, "begged" from others, or borrowed. They keep a running total of everything they bought on one side and how they paid for it on the other. The two sides have to balance, and that's why this record is called (wait for it....) the Balance Sheet.

Being smarter, faster, braver, or more photogenic does not show up on one's Balance Sheet - unless money changes hands. When one company buys another they pay extra for hard-to-quantify factors like street cred, customer lists, secret formulas, and talent. The fact that these intangible assets are called "Good Will" sort of makes sense.

But a whole lot about Balance Sheets does not make

sense. First, in the United States, assets are valued at what you paid for them. Got a great deal? Got suckered? The Balance Sheet just shows what you paid, good, bad, or ugly. If you've ever gotten anything stolen that was insured, your insurance company reimbursed you (after the damn deductible) for what you paid. Not what it was worth, or what it cost to replace. They asked for the receipt and that was it. Balance Sheet values work the same way - they are based on the receipt.

The part that doesn't make sense is that one's good will can't go up unless money changes hands. If you pay a dentist to cap your teeth, or if you line the pockets of acting schools, or buy each of your Nigerian children *Streethawker's Guide to The Galaxy* (just kidding!), you can increase your good will assets by the amount of all the receipts added together.

Speaking of good will, the decision to replenish ourselves with spectacular children certainly gets a lot of votes. More people will do that than will decide to brave a full theater with no idea what will happen the way we improvisers do.

What I'd like you to consider in thinking about the financial aspects of both decisions is that, whatever you decide, your decision will affect me and my decision will affect you.

Just please don't let your kids kick the back of my airplane seat!

Chapter Four

Should You Pick Up the Check?

From Each To Each, Keep That Cash A'Flowin'

Cash is good.
Cash is real.
Something you can touch.
*Something you can feel.**

It can feel really good to pick up the check - and really good to have someone else purposefully reach across the table and say, "My treat." And let's be honest. Who among us has not precisely timed a sojurn to the restroom to cross paths with the server holding that all-too-familiar leatherette envelope?

The point: the way you treat your cash, and that of others, is fraught with meaning.

I recently ran into a snafu with a member of my improvisational comedy troupe. We have a coaching session once a week. It costs $100 and we split it amongst us. While we've been together for several months now, we've just decided to get serious: hire a coach, commit to a weekly rehearsal, and work on marketing to build an audience. We met and all agreed on this, but our treasurer was away so no actual cash changed hands. Last week one person had a rough day and didn't show up for practice. I picked up the check for her on the rationale that:

- She knew we'd hired a coach, because she was at both the "agreement meeting" and last week's coaching and performance sessions.
- She definitely wants to be part of the troupe.

* A poem written by one of my students, a software engineer.

- I did not want our coach to have to collect it from her.
- I am the principal organizer.
- I have more money than she does.

This all looks very solid on paper and adds legitimacy to my request that she pay me back when we next meet to rehearse. But I was uncomfortable asking, fearing that I had somehow overstepped. Truth be told, I was a little angry at having to raise the issue in the first place, preferring that she pro-actively address it. Or better yet, just hand me a twenty.

Net net, I was worried that the way she treated the cash was indicative of how she felt about the group. Improv, like finance, is based on trust. It's an amorphous system that only works as long as we all believe in one another.

Could I trust her on the stage if I couldn't trust her in the pocketbook?

The Grameen Bank in India is the most famous example of using trust to build financial security – and vice-versa. They pioneered the concept of micro-enterprise lending. Women in a village get together and each kicks in a few rupees. Each week the total pot of about $4 goes to one vote-winning contender who promises to repay the money by a certain date. She buys things like a goat, part of a cell-phone, or craft supplies. Talk about social networking! Most years, more than 98% of the loans are paid back. The women are responsible in the up-close-and-personal sense, not to a faceless institution, but to the very countenances staring up at them each week. The way the money changes hands is a direct reflection of each woman's relationship to the group. Just as in my improv troupe, cash = commitment.

Heck, even Warren Buffett says, "The difference between a conversation and a commitment is a check."

So, back to the restaurant. Picking up the check signifies one or more of the following about the payer:

- They wish to make some kind of statement about their relationship to the non-payer.
- They have the cash (or at least the credit).
- They think it is their turn to spend it.

What about the other people at the table? Letting someone else pick up the check can be lovely - or anxiety-making. Why? Because it either implies a trade of some sort (your company for my money), or, if a trade doesn't take place, an imbalance of power. There, I said it. Cash = power. Not the only power, but one of the universally recognized kinds. Our use of cash mirrors our assumptions about our own power and that of others. Laying out cash makes us feel powerful - or exploited. Not laying out cash can make us feel holier-than-thou - or beholden.

I have been interested in the Co-operative Sector, of which the Grameen Bank is an iconic example, since I was in my teens. The whole idea of people involved in an enterprise together sharing financial power by "putting their money where their mouth is" is deeply appealing. But, like many ideas, it works better in theory than in practice. For the first co-op I was involved with, at the tender age of eighteen, the bugaboo was the sliding-scale-membership discussion.

Most of our members were white, middle-class young people. The co-op was in a neighborhood filled with non-white, non-middle-class, non-young people. We wanted them to shop at our store, a converted firehouse we renovated by hand. (My job was to fill in the grooves for the firetrucks with cement to make a smooth floor.) We discussed a sliding scale for membership dues, charging more money to those who had more and less money to those who had less. Sort of "from each according to his ability, to each according to his need" (Karl Marx, *Communist Manifesto*). Who am I kidding? More than "sort of"!

The problem occurred when we tried to define "ability" and "need." Is someone who could earn decent money but chooses not to earn it lacking in "ability" the same way an adult whose childhood was spent on welfare does? Does somebody with four children "need" a lower price for dried pinto beans than a single woman putting herself through college? Who has the right to judge another's ability and need? What if circumstances change and the former welfare recipient gets a great job? Do the words "ability" and "need" sound too zero-sum? We didn't like the idea of being locked into an "us vs. them" mentality. We were more attracted to the concept of ever-expanding resources based on encouraging generosity and openhandedness.

Finally, if we let people self-select, what will happen?

We can hardly offer a "conversation" or dried pinto beans to our landlord in lieu of a rent check. These discussions, fueled by a heated debate on whether to offer sugar-coated dried pineapple or the wizened, unsweetened variety, were where I cut my teeth (no pun intended) on the kind of economic anthropology that motivated this very book.

The concept of self-selection is fascinating. There is an all-you-can-eat vegetarian Indian buffet open only on Sundays that operates on a "pay what you think you owe" basis. The former print shop where our improv troupe performs also operates on this principle. We have tried "keep the lights on" appeals, as well as "suggested donations," but in both cases people, even those who can afford to pay more, usually don't. We all want to do what is fair, but this desire conflicts with the fear of getting played for a sucker.

The International Monetary Fund (IMF), acting in concert with various development banks, grapples with these same issues when they consider debt forgiveness to Third World countries. The IMF uses debt relief as a carrot to promote "poverty reduction and social policies." They provide interim debt relief and, "when a country meets its commitments, full debt-relief is provided," in the words of an IMF spokesperson.

The monologist Mike Daisey does something very interesting in his show, *The Last Cargo Cult*. As patrons enter, they are handed a bill - $1, $5, $10, or $20. During the show, which is about the strange values which capitalism can engender, Mr. Daisey tells us that we are, collectively, holding his fee in our hands. While he would like it back, it is up to us individually to do what we will with his money. Apparently, most people return it and some even throw in extra.

But before the IMF, our improv troupe, or Mr. Daisey decides whether to ask for contributions, rely on someone else to pay, or forgive a debt, somebody has to kick in the cash in the first place. There is no inherent fairness about who starts out in life with money or other resources. We cannot help where we were born, who we were born to, or our ancestral history. Many think that, economically speaking, biology is significantly contributive to destiny. However, what we can control is:

- What we do with the money that we touch.
- Where we choose to get more.
- Whether, when, and to whom we articulate our hopes, fears, and intentions.

Imagine the scene between two possibly-attracted co-workers:

"Want to come out for a drink after work?"

"Are you paying or am I?"

Kind of a romantic buzz-kill. What if the one inviting said:

"I'd like to buy you a drink after work."

Then the message is obvious, and the invitee has a choice. Or:

"Shall we go out after work and split the check?"

Again, intentions are much clearer if the invitation spells out the proposed financial relationship.

Taken to the logical extreme, a discussion about cash flow mirrors the power dynamics in any relationship.

This point is crystalized when we consider that cash for the bar tab, the improv coaching bill, the dried pineapple, and the IMF can only come from one of four places.

- Selling our precious life energy and hours on the planet.
- Selling or trading stuff we own.
- Borrowing using a buddy's generosity, your VISA, or the overdraft protection on your ATM or checking account.
- Begging. This is also called, puzzlingly, "raising equity" or "inheriting."

That's it. We do not cover printing money or stealing in this book. (The last line of the poem at the beginning of this chapter is "*something you can feel*" - not something you can steal!)

The person picking up the check can open his/her wallet, and take out the cash. It got there from one of the four ways listed above, but - and here's the kicker - the rest of us at the table typically have no idea how. Surprisingly, these four ways have very different causes and effects, although all can fatten your wallet. The next time you go to a restaurant, calculate how much of your time you had to sell to buy the flash-fried ginger calamari appetizer. If it costs $9.50, that is roughly an hour and a quarter of work at minimum wage (before accounting for taxes). So the person serving you the crispy calamari has to walk approximately two miles (one estimate reported that a server walks fifty miles in an eight-hour shift! While this is hopefully an exaggeration it should make you think), primarily spent carrying either a heavy tray or somebody else's dirty dishes, to afford the very calamari they are placing in front of you.

Rather than paying for the calamari by selling your time, you could have come up with the money by offering up something that you own. Try leaving a paperback book, or a plastic wastebasket, or a fancy pair of pantyhose sitting on the table in lieu of actual cash. The other two ways of paying the check (borrowing or begging) are covered by the prettiest word in the English language: *VISA* - or standing outside with your hat in your hand.

So - are you ready to pay the check now? More importantly, do you think that it is fair that you do? I have more money than the member of my improv troupe for whom I picked up the proverbial check. Does that mean it is fair that I pay? The adage "from each…to each" is not much different from the principles of supply and demand. In this case, I have the supply and they have the demand.

In case these questions seem perplexing, take heart in the reality that, so far, there is no fool-proof way to address them on a personal, national, or international scale. For example, the concept of currency valuation is just a "pay what you can" scheme writ large. When they were little, my kids came with me to all the countries I went to on business. We carried British pounds, German marks, Mexican pesos, Italian lira, French francs - and many others. They asked me, "Why isn't there just one kind of money?" I told them it had to do with perceptions of fairness and supply and demand.

Until 1933, the United States had a gold standard. All of our paper money was valued based on the amount of gold we had in our Treasury. The point of a gold standard was to get other countries to accept our money because it was insured, physically, by a precious metal. If dollars are expensive, and our goods are priced in dollars, they are too dear for foreigners to buy, so they shop elsewhere. China is having this problem now, as the yuan rises. It all started in 1944 at the Mt. Washington Hotel in Bretton Woods, New Hampshire, where representatives of forty-four countries got together and fixed the price at which countries could exchange their currencies for gold (it was $35 per ounce).

This was the beginning of the International Monetary Fund. Instead of gold we could have used tin or diamonds, coal or Walt Whitman's first editions. In fact, silver standards were common in the 1800s.

The US dumped the gold standard because we were doing too much international trade, and because gold was, ironically, getting too precious. This idea was abandoned in 1971 when the price of gold, and the currencies tied to it, were un-coupled and left to "float." Countries were free to let the world value their currencies, essentially to "pay what you want." These decisions are made on complex and ever-changing definitions of what is fair, and safe, and good, and show in the value of a country's currency and in the interest rate they must pay to borrow money.

Since 1971 countries have experimented with finding standards for their currency to help buyers measure risk, on the theory that this will avoid bingey-purgey cycles. Examples are the Euro, and Argentina pegging its peso to the US dollar. I will never forget putting my ATM card into a slot across from the big opera house in Buenos Aires and being asked whether I wanted dollars or pesos. Poorer counties, which the world thinks will have trouble paying back their debts, have "soft" currencies. Richer countries have "hard" currencies, but this is just a way of expressing the "from each/to each" mentality. The *Wall Street Journal* (Aug 10, 2010) said, "One old economist's saw says that the higher a nation's intelligence and moral strength, the lower its rate of interest."

Is the "from each/to each" idea also the reason we tip the waiter and not the doctor or lawyer? Is it because the doctor and lawyer are "professionals" and thus of a higher class? Is it because they usually get higher salaries because anybody can wait a table but not anyone can remove an appendix (or sue if the operation goes awry)? Or is it because restaurant owners count on tips to make up for the fact that they do not want to pay waitstaff enough to buy their own flash-fried ginger calamari?

Is the concept of "from each/to each" truly more fair? As I think about it, there really is not much difference between an ability and a need. Doesn't lack of ability equal need? Is ability self-determined and need inherited? Vice-versa? Who really deserves to eat unsweetened pineapple anyway? My brain hurts... The real question is, "who gets to decide?" And, once they do, how do they enforce it?

So pick up the check - or don't. Tip your waiter - or your doctor. Pay in services or stuff or credit. But remember: cash is a mirror of your power.

Chapter Five

The Answer Is *(Drumroll Please!)* ...$150,000

Over my career many people have asked how much money they need to live out their old age. Some of them read scary articles predicting the death of Social Security. Others get hoodwinked by their financial planners into using retirement planning software. These programs thoughtfully inform every single person who touches them, in meticulous detail...that they are going to be eating dog food when they're sixty-five. The only way to avoid competing with Fido is (you guessed it) to immediately hand over every penny to . . . the financial planners themselves.

In finance, as in improv, there are few cut-and-dried answers. There is no one thing that works for everybody, unless it's embracing that awful feeling of being off-balance that tends to force maximum creativity. But, in my humble opinion, the Answer to how much you need to save to live out the rest of your life is immutable.

Once the kids are through college (at the latest), all you need to have is $150,000 safely squirrelled away for emergencies. Divide the $150,000 in two and buy two Certificates of Deposit (CDs). Banks sell these. Choose two banks you like and buy one from each.

CDs work like this. You fork over your money in increments as small as $1,000 and agree to let them keep it for a defined period, usually between six months and two years. They then take your money and lend it to somebody else for, say, a mortgage. The person with the mortgage (hopefully) pays the bank back at a higher interest rate than they pay to you for the use of their money. Certificates of Deposit are insured by the Federal government in amounts up to $250,000. If the banks fail, the government agrees to pay you back your money. This has actually happened in isolated instances in recent years. The system works as long as most banks stay solvent. If you are concerned that most banks won't be solvent, then you definitely want to spend your excess money now!

Spend the rest now. I dare you!

Here are the reasons why $150,000 in an emergency fund is all you need.

First, $150,000 is a lot of money. It should last the normal person at least eighteen months, during which time you can figure out the next thing to do if it's a real crisis. When estimating how much you actually need to live, take your food budget and multiply by three. If you want to be über-careful, multiply by seven. (These figures are from sources used to estimate the poverty line.) How much more than that do you really need? Adam Smith (*Wealth of Nations*) said, "Social embarrassment plays a part in determining necessity." Do you really want to spend your life guarding against social embarrassment?

On the other hand, maybe you should take old Adam at his word and seek out social embarrassment. Perhaps that's just my improv training talking. Few things are more "socially embarrassing" than standing up in front of a bunch of people who are expecting you to make them laugh!
Most people have a whole lot less than $150,000 by

the time they retire. In fact, according to the Employee Benefit Retirement Institute, 43% of Americans don't even have $10,000 over and above Social Security or their employer retirement fund. Most (54%, according to Fidelity Investments) have less than $25,000, counting everything.

Second, more savings will not protect you from everything. You have no idea what kind of shape you or the world will be in when you hit traditional retirement age. You may have the desire and ability to keep earning enough money to live on until the day your toes turn up. Saving more and more and more is a sucker's game cooked up by the financial services industry to line their own pockets. There's a good chance in any short to mid-term period that you could lose it all, probably just when you need it the most. My own broker tried to convince me to give him my retirement contribution to put into the stock market in 2008. Had I taken his advice, every penny would have been gone by early 2009 when the Dow hit a twelve-and-a-half-year low.

Instead of saving on their own, many people use 401Ks (employer-sponsored programs) to salt cash away for retirement. The idea of a 401K is that people put money in them during their higher earning years and take it out during their lower earnings years. The implicit assumptions are:

A) Retirement age = lower earnings + lower expenses (which in combination = more money in your pocket)

and

B) Lower earnings = smaller tax bite

Neither of these assumptions may turn out to be anything close to true! When you're "retirement age" you could well have higher earnings, and/or higher expenses. And there is no guarantee that taxes will be lower! Last year, British people earning over £150,000 saw their maximum tax rate go up to 50%. By the way, during WWII, the top British tax rate was (wait for it...) 99.25%. By 1973 it had fallen to (only) 75%, but let us not feel sorry that John Lennon had to move to the Dakota in New York City. We can feel plenty sorry about what happened later, but that's another story.

Many people over-save to guard against the financial impact of a catastrophic illness or accident. Standard hospitalization costs about $2,000 per day – intensive care costs between $1,000 and $3,500 per day. Just getting an ambulance can easily cost $500. Chronic illnesses such as diabetes cost $7,500 (in 2007), and nearly one-third of terminally ill patients with insurance use up most or all of their savings to cover uninsured medical expenses such as home care. No matter how much money you save over my magic $150,000 you can't save enough to afford a health catastrophe and continue any kind of normal life.

And that is why (I hope) you have health insurance! Hospitals actually charge you MORE without it, but that is a subject above my pay grade.

Third, you might be better off spending your money

now. Even if you have extra money when you retire you may not be able to use it the way you could in your younger years. You may be sick, too tired, or both. You may be interested in living much more frugally, in the Peace Corps, in a commune - or an assisted living community that wants all your assets. Spending money later just might not be as satisfying as spending it all today.

But what about the kids, you ask? Well, the kids might need financial help now. Barring the need for long-term medical assistance, wouldn't it be a whole lot more satisfying for both you and them to be able to see the new house you helped them buy? Hear about the great trip you funded? Hand over the keys to the car they want but can't afford? Showering adult children with significant amounts of inherited money isn't even good for them (see *Rich Dad, Poor Dad* if you have any questions about why I say this). And, on a larger scale, keeping up the tradition of inherited wealth continues to promote social stratification of the worst kind. So please, don't tell me you can't be satisfied spending the money now because the kids will need it later.

Speaking of satisfaction, or lack of same, you may be in a job you hate, just working to make enough to save for retirement. Saddest thing I ever heard. People in jobs they hate get smaller and smaller and meeker and meeker. At the end of every day they have less of themselves than they had when they started. If you knew you *only had to save $150,000, what would your life be like now?*

For those readers out there who do like their jobs and

are looking for a way to spend the extra money, my hands-down favorite thing to buy is increased brain function. I don't care whether you collect art (shoes are art!), go to a shrink, take a vacation, see a nutritionist, or sign up at the gym. Go back to school, get a books-on-tape membership, or pay the babysitter so you can sit and read. Hey! Come and see my troupe do improv. In my opinion, fully half of your savings over $150,000 should get reinvested in that space between your ears.

My next favorite use of extra money is helping yourself by helping others. But make sure you are doing it in that order. (See Chapter Seven, "If You Give A Mouse A Cookie.")

But the most important reason not to save too much is that we are all, to varying degrees, cowards. The decision about what to do with our money is too frightening to make, so we just keep saving and saving without ever being brave enough to decide. Take Japan. Until recently, the average Japanese person saved 11.2% of his disposable income (in the US we are lucky to be saving half that), when banks paid *zero* percent interest on savings accounts. Zero! Banks weren't lending, so they weren't collecting interest. Consequently they chose not to pay it out. This caused "stagflation," which basically means the economy was turgid, and innovation suffered.

I was once privy to a conversation among young adults, all of whom were filthy rich, having been gifted by their parents. I will never forget how movingly one woman talked about what she experienced just opening the mail. Beset by endless heart-wrenching pleas for donations, a goodly number of which she was in a position to grant, she was terrified to make the wrong choice. She felt responsible, in no small way, for the misfortune of others. So she agonized constantly and never felt satisfied that she was doing enough. The money she'd inherited became a burden.

Right now lots of you are saying, "I'd love to have that kind of a burden!" Look for a minute at lottery winners who became "over-saved" overnight. Some financial experts estimate that 70% are worse off after they win the money than before. Many choose to change their names! The ones who are successful buy themselves one or two expensive gifties and then continue to lead their normal lives.

The heavy burden of fear, and its companion, cowardice, show up in the improv world all the time. Remember, in improv, everything is all made up. The goal is to be open, throw yourself right out there, and see what happens. This is, at least for me, completely terrifying. Last night, for example, I was convinced I was going to hurl, even before I walked into the theater.

When improvisers are scared we freeze. We flounder around. We pander for cheap laughs. We become clichés.

You see this in the "cowboy" stance that opens all too many a scene. One person walks out, standing at a forty-five-degree angle to the audience. They are alone. Time passes. They are still alone. They remain alone. Finally, somebody else decides that enough is enough, enters and takes a position at just the same angle. There is a triangle of space between them. They look like two cowboys assessing a stubborn mule. The scene is effectively dead right then and there. Shot through the heart.

The other thing we improvisers do when we get scared is drop our character's motivation and steal the juice from our scene partners. Last night I was proud of myself - I stuck to my guns. My character, a company newsletter-writer named Laurene, had a thick Southern accent, a submissive posture, and very big eavesdroppy ears. She was desperately seeking the approval and respect of her co-workers. Laurene would have settled for mere tolerance but even that was a faraway dream. Playing her - all "Puhleeze laahk me! Puhleeze!" was disturbingly close to the real me on bad days, but I stuck with it and kept heightening her desperation until a panic attack ensured. Had I wimped out, I would have had Laurene pretend she didn't care - or change her tack entirely and start bossing people around.

Scared improvisers also fly into the arms of culturally recognized archetypes. When we're on a watercraft it's always a submarine and we play the lookout lowering the periscope. In a classroom scene, nine times out of ten the teacher is hitting on a student. When we are at a party we're always having a gay awakening. I cannot tell you the number of scenes I've seen about high school where every character was a mirror image of somebody in *The Breakfast Club*.

Cowardly improvisers fail themselves and their

troupe. Worse, the audience gets ripped off. They came to see real life the way it should be on the stage and want to laugh at the funny things that people do all the time. They are left paying to watch other people be afraid.

Cowardly over-s*avers* also fail themselves and their posses. Failure to be brave, take risks, and use one's money now guarantees the most boring choices and thus the least investment in art, in beauty, in family, and in community. It also tanks the economy big time.

So, if you have over $150,000 and the kids are through with college (yes, I think college has to be paid for first), then take the extra money and make a choice. In finance, as in improv, the worst thing you can do is just stand there.

Chapter Six

Kill the Cars

I wanted to do a chapter on cars because I find the whole subject fascinating, as in watching a child pull the wings off a butterfly. If I had my druthers we would walk out our doors, program our transportation pods, and be zoomed in safe and private comfort to our destinations. Were I ready to fully embrace time travel, I'd just say "Beam me up, Scotty" and get there even faster. But hey, I'm just not *that* flexible.

Once I read a story in which the author looked down from Mars and thought that the Earth was created to serve the Almighty Car. That opinion served only to underscore mine: I hate cars.

I hate cars because I feel trapped in a ton of metal hurtling too fast, separated from other drivers doing god-knows-what by thin little school-bus-yellow lines that somebody painted on the road. If I am in a car for longer than, say, forty-five minutes I become suddenly ravenous or parched. And develop a desperate need to go to the bathroom. All the gizmos are confusing, and I feel stupid for not intuitively knowing how to roll down the window, turn on the radio, or adjust the mirrors. Then there is the traffic, which I am helpless to control, cope with, or even understand.

Even without traffic, I tend to get lost, and, depending upon my state of mind, cannot comprehend even the simplest of directions. I hate anyone who tells me to take the bridge over the underpass. How can you drive over an underpass? Makes no sense at all. Even with a GPS admonishing me to turn in five hundred feet I can take the wrong ramp. Then I have to listen to a nasty, puzzlingly British voice telling me she is recalculating. There was a recent news story about an elderly couple with dementia who got disoriented driving home from a familiar place, ended up in a farmer's field somewhere and froze to death. In a few years I fear that could be me!

As a finance person, I hate cars even more. I am suspicious of the ads, with all their small print. I am suspicious of the salespeople with their fancy clothes and big gold jewelry. And when cars break, as they always do, I am suspicious of the repair people. In summary, cars make me a combination of helpless and dependent. Throw in the fact that they cost vast sums of money and you have the motivation for this chapter.

Don't get me wrong, I am all for blowing a wad. Just ask me about my eBay...But, given that cars are usually purchased using debt, they are a colossal waste of coin.

Over your lifetime, you could well spend more on cars than you will on housing. This is scary. What makes it scarier is that one always goes down while the other has a chance to go up. Add the debt financing aspect (i.e., mortgage and car loan) and the situation worsens. The exception to this is you Californians, who may well spend more of your waking hours in your car than in your house. It seems to me that many Californians actually live in their cars (check the fast food wrappers in the back seat), but that's a different story.

We all have to live somewhere and we all have to use transportation. This chapter will hopefully help you get the most for your money. Some years ago, a boss of mine, whom I will call Jessica Beauregard Williamsburg, once bought a blood-red Ferrari convertible to celebrate winning a big deal. No, that's wrong. She bought it to motivate herself to win the next big deal. The thing cost upwards of $50,000. This is a woman who believed that pretty packaging can be more important than the gift that is inside - and, being terrifically intelligent, she was probably right. Anyway, she bought the Ferrari. But she did not drive the Ferrari, at least not very often. Because it could get rained on. Or snowed on. Or splashed with mud. There was nowhere suitably covered, heated/cooled, and attended to safely entrust it, even for an hour, that was close enough to her meetings. So the $50,000 investment became a candy wrapper in which to present herself to her much-younger boyfriend, who happened (and I am not making this up) to be an arms dealer in southern Virginia. My boss probably spent upwards of $100 per mile - not a great use of her money!

Cars, like improv, can do things that nothing else can do. A car is your personal, private accessory. Your car waits patiently for you to turn it on, and is available to you 24/7. People use vanity plates, bumper stickers, custom spoilers, roof graphics, and hubcaps to communicate everything from their sexual availability to their alma mater to their politics. Given proper care and maintenance, your beloved vehicle can go hundreds of thousands of miles, completely at your necessity or whim. Plenty of people could not get to their jobs, pick up and deliver their kids, or even buy groceries without a car. Car ownership lets you transport your loved ones, co-workers, or even (still) the occasional hitch-hiker. Who can forget that new-driver feeling of freedom?

Improv also knows no boundaries in space and time. Last night's show featured a couple who took up residence on the back of an altruistic sea turtle. Scenes can feature one person, eight people, or only a disembodied voice from the wings (as in when I played God to a Jonah-like sad sack). Props are mimed, and your fellow actors can do "scene painting" to provide context. While you're performing, say, a hospital scene, other troupe members can rush in and say things like, "We see this hospital is in Bhutan," causing the doctor to adjust your happiness IV.

Improv, by its very nature, is evanescent. Based entirely on the powerful combo of audience good will and actors' bravery, imagination, and teamwork, it is the ultimate "you had to be there" performance art form. Makes lousy TV, except as filler for sketch and stand-up comedy. Like your car, improv is a purpose-built machine. It can do things no other art form can.

Unlike your car, improv doesn't depreciate. Once I was working in a DC exurb near Dulles Airport. It was a baking hot summer day, the kind that garnered federal workers hardship pay in the early 19th century. I glanced out the window and saw probably two acres of cars depreciating before my very eyes. The blast-furnace known as the Sun was fading the paint, swelling the tires, singeing the upholstery, and boiling the water that was supposed to cool the engine. Here's a fun fact – you only use the car 5% of the time you own it. My boss, Ms. Beauregard somepin' somepin', used her Ferrari much less than even that. Same deal with your car. So, to review:

- You can spend more on your car than your house or apartment.
- You go in hock to buy it.
- Unless you're Jerry Seinfeld your "investment"only goes down, and rapidly.
- You only use it about 5% of the time.

Now I'll make it worse. Your car is more likely to hurt or kill you than anything, or anyone, you come in contact with, even for those who do not drive. You are much more likely to die in a car accident than in a plane crash, natural disaster, or terrorist attack.

About 14% of the average person's taxes go to street and highway infrastructure and parking which is largely used by cars. We live in inner-city DC and the parking police, AKA bounty hunters, I swear, must have a condo on our street. They have also perfected the Invisibility Cloak (which plays such an important role in *Harry Potter and the Deathly Hallows*) because they materialize just as someone leaves their car for a sec to pick up their prescription or take-out order, then dematerialize before the hapless parker comes back to find a $30 ticket and vents his rage with the ice-scraper. This performance has got to be expensive, and we are all paying for it, drivers and non-drivers alike.

Car-generated pollution is also very expensive, costing about five cents per driver per mile, and that's not counting the ozone layer. Then there is noise pollution and the physical harm to bicycle messengers to consider.

The furthest-out thinkers add up the costs of our economic dependence on foreign oil and come up with a figure, in 2005 dollars, of seven trillion since 1970. This is about $20,000 per person, and doesn't count the political risk of having waaay too many people in the Middle East not in love with Americans. There was even a short-lived TV show, called *Rubicon*, about this very subject, and it did feature a twenty-something man, strapped to a bomb. Just sayin'.

So, still think cars are an "asset"? The word "asset" in finance does not mean good, only that you have bought something which is likely to be physical, lasts more than a year, and costs more than (usually) $1,000. Assets are also known as "capital expenditures." They always require asset's evil twin, called "operating expenses," and in the case of cars that means gas, oil, maintenance, time. None of these downsides is portrayed in TV car ads, which tend to feature a troubling co-dependence with sporting events and beer commercials.

Car ads during the (American) football playoffs promise "Unequaled Inspiration," say "Good Morning, Innovation," and "When You Lead Others Follow." They reassure viewer/buyers that "You Have Nothing to Hide," ask, "What Happened to Luxury?," then answer their own question by presenting us with "Luxury With Lightning In Its Veins."

Okay, maybe most non-urbanites need a car. But do

they need the car they have? Maybe you're lured by the car commercials referenced above. Can't you see yourself behind the wheel of an (insert here) Miata, Cadillac, or Jaguar? Lots of people can. But, as my mother used to say, your eyes are bigger than your stomach. This disturbing gap – between what you want and what you need - is handily closed by a financial tool called leasing.

Leasing is a type of financing whereby you don't actually own the asset, you just buy the right to use it. It is different than buying things, like houses, or couches, or prom dresses, where the seller lets you pay for the asset over time, but you still own it. Department stores love when you purchase things on their store credit card, then don't pay the credit card balance right away. That lets them charge you interest on what you bought, at annual percentage rates over 15%. As long as you pay the card balance eventually, they are ecstatic. And you get the prom dress well before you actually could have afforded to buy it. So in a sense, everybody wins.

Leasing companies assume you do not want to own the asset, at least not right away. Car leasing is a particularly sweet spot. Before the auto industry crashed, and probably all during it come to think, car manufacturers made much more profit on car lease interest than they did on actual cars.

Car leasing appeals to people who have to, just *have* to have a new car at least every three years. They are willing to pay up to 15% more just for the privilege of:

- That new car feeling as described so poetically above,
- Not having to worry about the car breaking down,
- Being able to turn it in at the end of the lease and start the whole cycle over again; which means
- They can experiment with convertibles, hybrids, sedans; and
- Change the color of the car to match their hair color or what's new for autumn. (Hint: chocolate brown is finally out).

Sounds good? Car leasing companies are not charities designed to bring joy to millions. They load all kinds of internal costs onto lease prices and just pray that the low-low-low monthly payment lulls the lessor into swallowing them. Lease payments generally include:

- Interest on the money the car company had to borrow to get the vehicle on the lot in the first place,
- All the depreciation on the asset over its entire "useful life" front loaded into the lease period,
- Costs to collect and process all the lease payments from everyone, including those who do not pay (sort of like an employer-sponsored health insurance pool. Healthy people pay for every back surgery, high-risk delivery, and dialysis treatment. Only leasing is not a social good), and . . .
- Profit for the leasing company.

Those who lease cars also have limits on how many miles they can drive, and are required to maintain the car to specific standards. This is so the leasing company can sell the car at the the end of the lease and make their real money. Do me a favor and never, ever buy "your" car at the end of its lease. If you do, you are paying extra for huge amounts of flexibility which you did not use. People who do not succumb to car lease ads, or who can innoculate themselves with this chapter, buy these gently used, barely driven, fully depreciated, beautifully maintained automobiles at the end of someone else's lease. That's a good thing.

The premise of leasing is that anything is affordable as long as the monthly payments are low. This is the same rationale that causes otherwise sane people to buy boats (BOAT = Break Out Another Thousand).

So, buying a car is financially unsound, and so is leasing. Still, many people need a car. The issue once again comes down to this: do you need the car, or cars, you have? I recommend that you ask yourself, "What is the Point of a Car?" There are three answers: transportation (which includes safety and comfort), investment, and ego. Assign a percentage to each category, making the percentages add to 100%. If transportation is at the top of your list, buy an inexpensive car and work hard to understand how it works so you can do simple maintenance yourself. Pay cash. If this blows your budget, pick up a babied car coming off someone else's lease.

If you gave any weight to investment and you are not a car collector, you're dreaming, so cross it out. Those of you who quantified your ego involvement, extra points from me for blasting yourself out of denial.

Given that most of you will own a car, here is how to make the best use of your money:

- Make sure you know why you own the car in the first place. If it is for ego gratification, rent a really fancy vehicle a couple of times a month, otherwise
- Buy a two-year-old car for cash. Shell out for a vanity plate, fancy hubcaps, or a hood ornament instead of a new vehicle. You can even purchase a new-car-smell fragrance spray.
- Maintain the car perfectly, and schedule work in advance. This will require finding a great mechanic. It is worth it.
- Forget you know how to spell the word "lease."
- Consider the total cost of ownership. This includes parking, tickets, and the cost to tow yourself back from wherever the car broke down because you didn't maintain it.

Despite my obvious car hatred, I do believe that your car, like your clothes, investment portfolio, charitable giving, and state of the sock drawer, should reflect *you*, and what you believe in.

This is why dealers run out of Priuses.

Now, back to my eBay habit…

Chapter Seven

Should You Give a Mouse a Cookie?

Donating and Receiving Financial Charity

Should You Give a Mouse a Cookie? This popular children's book by Laura Numeroff recounts the insatiable needs of an adorable yet not-entirely-well-meaning young mouse. First, he wants a cookie, then some milk to go with it, then a straw, a napkin, etc. etc., until he gets hungry again and asks for . . . another cookie. The unseen wish-granter keeps giving and giving and giving, with no end in sight.

This charming exercise in circular logic mirrors the decisions we all face when deciding whether, when, how much, and with whom we wish to exchange charitable gifts. For all of us, from time to time, will be on the giving and receiving end of financial charity. Some charity will be among members of our family, others between us and non-profit organizations. Let's start with my operating premise that all the money in the world is connected, just like all the water. Money flows from person to person, group to group, and country to country, just as condensation draws water into the clouds until it rains and falls to the seas. At any one time, some parts of the world are flooding and others are parched. To a large degree it is just luck that most of us manage to avoid extremes.

Because they have to do with money, charitable giving and receiving are also connected. We can control some of the giving and receiving directly, making our experience up close and personal. But most of the charitable giving and receiving is through the tax system, which we can only control through political action. Unless you wish to go to jail for tax dodging, political action is, at best, frustratingly diffuse and peripatetic. Other than in the voting booth, none of the governmental charitable taking and giving is under our individual control.

First fact: everyone reading this is getting charity. If you own a home in the United States you enjoy a tax deduction for the interest. If you have a high income, President George W. Bush gave you a tax break. If you send your child to public school, everyone, including those without children and those whose children do not even use the public schools, charitably pays for it. If you live on a military base, your food and basic supplies are subsidized at the PX by those who are not eating the food or using the supplies. If you receive disability from the government, everyone else is paying for it regardless of their abilities.

What is the difference, then, between charity and societal benefits? Both act as a counterweight to capitalism, preventing the marketplace victor from claiming every last scrap of the spoils. Both reflect changing norms. Both assume one person's gain comes at the expense of another's loss. Interestingly, there is an implicit sense of expanded self-worth connected to giving charity, even though few of us feel proud to pay taxes. Shame is often connected to receiving charity, while few are ashamed to claim deductions.

So, unless you want to move to the Cayman Islands where there is no income tax, charitable giving and receiving is defined here as those financial interchanges which we can most closely control.

Some of the giving and taking happens between family members and friends. Here's where the mouse/

cookie story comes most clearly into play.

Many people within families financially support one another. Some posit that long-term financial support is one reason people have families in the first place. Before the US Industrial Revolution the average family size was much larger than it is today. Given infant mortality, lots of children were needed to work in the fields. Birth rates fall all over the world as economies rise, and rise when economies fall.

The idea that families exist as a sort of financial safety net is satisfying and horrible - at the same time. Satisfying because financial support is a fairly reliable way to show love and commitment. Horrifying because intra-familial financial decisions cannot fail to be encrusted with emotional baggage. Money becomes yet another tool to express power dynamics. Taking the time to define rationally what is "good" or even "fair" for both parties is frowned upon (try asking for a prenup). And the consequences of poor decisions get passed down from generation to generation.

Take the case of my friend, Cindy. Her sister is beset by mental illness and spends many days unable to get out of bed. Cindy is concerned for her nieces, who have rarely known the feeling of being safe. Teenage girls have a lot of dangerous ways to make themselves feel safer, and Cindy is trying to head trouble off at the pass.

Her eldest niece, Paige, has just dropped out of high school and is going down the tubes fast. Cindy has decided to help Paige get out of her toxic family environment and into boarding school. She is planning to foot the bill, is driving her to all her school interviews, and has even bought her a new dress. Then comes the inevitable.

First, Paige does not complete her applications. So Cindy helps her. Then one of her at-home teachers reveals that Paige has not done homework for months. So Cindy intervenes to help work out a resolution that doesn't tank Paige's grades.

Now comes the hard part – the school Paige wants to go to costs a whole lot of money, close to a third of Cindy's annual take-home pay. Cindy is concerned that once she gets into the role of Sugar Aunt she will be looking at nearly a decade of educational expenses. And travel. And clothing. And health care. And Paige has a younger sister...

It may seem bizarre, but my advice to Cindy was simple: "Take back more than you give."

If Cindy gave and gave and gave she would have no money left. Even if all the money in the world is connected, it would likely take a long time for resources to flow her way. Bankrupting herself would not be in anyone's best interests, Paige included.

Instead, Cindy could ensure that she takes as much as she gives. She could start by examining her motives for wanting to help Paige. Is it out of duty? Benevolence? Guilt? Lots of money changes hands based on guilt. Direct mail marketers know this. The outside of one envelope I just received shows a desperate little girl with a cleft palate and a hungry face. Another inquires whether I'm deeply aware of genocide in Darfur. A third tells me it is up to me personally to save the polar bears. I am not that big on polar bears.

Next, Paige could be told how much her school is costing Cindy, both in absolute dollars and in percentage-of-salary-terms. She needs to see that she is costing Cindy one fabulous world cruise. Or one silver Lexus RX per year. Or the satisfaction of investing in a local restaurant. Or three years of interest on the mortgage.

Paige would also be served by realizing that accepting Cindy's kind offer has a price. Receiving charity will actually cost her – in time, money, and psychic obligations. Is there a limit to those obligations? When will the "debt" be repaid? How will the inevitable resentment (from both parties) be addressed?

Both Cindy and Paige need to figure out how, and when, the debt will be repaid. Can Paige create artwork to grace the living room? House-sit or shop and cook during school vacations? Work hard and earn a scholarship? Pass the charity on to someone else through tutoring or mentoring others?

Both parties could discuss whether, and under what conditions, Cindy will fork over more dough.

And all of this, every scrap, needs to be written down.

The popular book *Rich Dad, Poor Dad* by Robert Kiyosaki and Sharon Lecter makes the point that those who inherit wealth usually pay for it in terms of directionless lives fraught with avoidable problems. Yet the alternative, not leaving money to one's children, is also painful. Deciding whether or not to accept charity is also a slippery slope. The goal, in my humble opinion, is to find the right balance. If donors make sure they take more than they give and receivers make sure to give more than they take, nobody will be flooded and nobody will be parched.

Outside of charity between family members, voluntary giving and taking also exists between individuals and institutions. In fact, most of the charity in the United States takes place between poor people and their churches. The average low-income person gives away a much higher percentage of his income than does the average millionaire. Non-profits are huge business, representing $1.4 trillion in the US alone. Why do they exist?

There are at least two opposing theories about why the non-profit sector exists, one positive and one negative. The happy story line is that non-profits serve a vital purpose in society. The government can never do everything (and we don't want it to, especially in the case of funding churches) so individuals are compensated in the form of tax deductions for supporting institutions which can best fill in the gaps. Gaps get plugged by experts, and individual donors have a long list of good causes to choose from. This gives us all a much-needed sense of control over our destiny, and allows us to create individual giving plans which reflect our priorities. My recently deceased father wrote fifty checks the last month he was alive; for $10 each. Some of his choices - Veterans of Foreign Wars, Boys Town, the Blind VA Association, Vietnam Veterans of America - made sense, and reflected who he was and what moved him. Of course the very fact that he wrote fifty checks tells us he may have been losing his marbles, but that is another story.

The unhappy story is that non-profits are safety valves, designed to ameliorate just enough egregious pain and suffering so the status quo - and the growing gap between rich and poor - can keep chugging along. Act Two of this story says that the only way The Revolution will come is when people reach their limit, and that non-profits are designed to make sure that never happens. This theory is supported by the fact that the vast majority of non-church non-profit funding comes from the rich people on the other side of the barricades. What is the best way to determine whether, how, and how much to give and to take? Could your participation be causing more harm than good?

It takes at least $25 to solicit and process a donation, maintain records of the donor, and keep that donation on the books. So if last month was the first and only time my Dad chose to support Boys Town he actually cost Father Flanagan money. And, as you all know, the minute you make a donation, what do you get back? A thank you note which thoughtfully includes a stamped self-addressed envelope in which you are encouraged to send back...yet another donation.

My seventeen-year-old son is being recruited to play soccer in college. He has been asked by at least thirty coaches to attend their camp and visit their school. We've been advised to evaluate all offers using the "Broken Leg" test. This criterion is: in the unlikely event of a career-ending injury would you still want to be at that school? My version of this when applied to charitable giving is "If you became a recipient of this organization's largess would you be willing to pay it back?"

The best charities are significantly funded, in time if not in money, by the people whom they wish to help. A good example is the newspaper, *Street Sense*, which is written and then sold by homeless people. A bad example is a "community-based," "grass-roots" non-profit that's funded by a couple of rich people.

The best charities for you to ally with are ones where you donate time as well as money and interact with the recipients. I work in a childrens' literacy program at the elementary school on my corner two days a week. There is no argument that I get back more than I give. And Sergio's and Yesenia's and Jessica's gain does not come at the expense of any loss on my part whatsoever!

The best charities for you to fund are those that make your actual world better. Choose ones where you can see the impact of your donation up close and personal. Take as much as you give and keep the money flowing.

If you are receiving governmental benefits or tax advantages, know their economic value and be grateful. You may have already paid them back, or not. If you are receiving charity now, start to pay it back any way you can, just like Paige in the story above. Make yourself aware of how much you owe and who is paying. That way you can determine when the debt has been paid.

And, just for the general karmic benefit, everyone should send some money, even a little, to people who got caught by fate on the wrong side of the barricades. Because someday it will be your turn. Who gets and who gives is, at the end, just a question of timing.

Chapter Eight

Is Running a Non-Profit a Good Career Move? What About an Improv Troupe?

Many non-profits do good, sometimes life-changing work. Our world would be a lesser place without the blood the Red Cross delivers, or the lawsuits Southern Poverty Law Center files, or the houses that Habitat for Humanity builds. Helping others engenders positive feelings and sparks inspirational acts. Being in the company of those who share a common goal of service can create a life filled with purpose.

But, and I am not trying to be smarmy here, most non-profits should not exist. They are essentially vanity presses created to assuage guilt, and there are way too many guilty people. Non-profits can end up patronizing those they are designed to help. They tend to mirror, and sometimes exacerbate, the very problems they were created to address. Worst, they never help enough because they don't want to put themselves out of business. Their very existence takes pressure off public services who many think should be the ones working on social problems. Despite that the non-profit sector in the United States has grown one hundred percent since 1940, not much has really changed.

In the same vein, most improv troupes should die. They tend to get hide-bound, cliquish, and unbelievably judgmental. If the point of improv is to awaken the creative genius in oneself and others, anybody ought to be able to do it. Yet auditioning one's way into a troupe depends upon being accepted by the other members of the troupe who, in my experience, choose people who don't make them uncomfortable by calling into question their very existence.

Improv troupes are almost always connected to Theaters, which in turn rely on their schools to survive. It is entirely possible for an improv school to take your money for years and never let you onto a house troupe. You can take classes until your teeth fall out, as Mick Napier puts it in his seminal work *Improvise,* but the only way to get better is to perform. The only way to perform is to make (or found) a troupe. The people in house troupes make what little money their art provides teaching classes run by improv schools. They all play on each other's troupes and rarely let anyone else in. Sadly, bitterly, this makes the inherent promise of improv - creative genius expansion - a baldfaced lie. Oxymoron is perhaps a kinder word. Color me bitter.

Running a successful non-profit, or an improv troupe, depends on planning to shoot yourself in the head so you can go on and do the next thing - and leave room for other people to take a turn. My point is that there is a natural lifecycle and we should all respect it. The key to running a successful anything is to define success, then perform ritual *seppuku* when you achieve it. I once read an article about Japanese innovation. Just as death is a part of life, product development cycles are designed to include a "kill it" phase.

Defining "success" is a whole lot harder than it sounds, because success requires trade-offs. Trade-offs take guts, but they are harder to make in non-profits than for-profits because non-profits hide behind a veil of financial holiness. In the for-profit or private sector, using financial metrics to define "success" is accepted as mandatory. In the non-profit world it is too often considered distasteful and off-message. This makes answering the question, "When can we declare victory?" a whole lot tougher.

Is a non-profit tutoring organization successful when standardized test scores improve? When fewer kids get sent to the principal for bad behavior? When obesity rates fall? Is an improv troupe successful when audiences increase? When the "love and respect" jar we use at our performing venue has a lot of money in it? When we all take the next steps in our lives? Answering "all of the above" doesn't cut it!

Real success is not only hard to define but depressing to contemplate. Setting goals means focusing on outcomes and not just process. I have a friend who wants to combine psychotherapy with spirituality to help people live fuller lives. In her heart of hearts she thinks most people are just too far gone to be healthy. She thinks that once we grow up (and probably the cut-off is about four) we are who we are. We can get a little better on the margins but not really move forward. In my opinion, most social change efforts are doomed to fail. And most improvisers can't or won't really be able to connect with themselves and one another well enough to be good on stage. The real question is, *Are there points for trying?*

I say yes, but only if somebody is brave enough to set goals that aim in the right direction. Here is a list of Key Performance Indicators (KPIs) from the newsletter *Non-Profit Fiscal Fitness*, October 2004. Goals are sorted into financial, process, customer, and learning/growth categories.

Financial KPIs

- Cash flow ($)
- Cost per dollar raised ($)
- Cost per service offered ($)
- Contributions in dollars or units for a given period
- Collection rates and amounts by funding source
- Average gift amount by age range
- Average gift amount by gift type
- Proportion of October contributions to total annual donations

Process KPIs

- Improvement in productivity (%)
- Administrative expense ($)
- Cost of administrative errors ($)
- Average length of time to process a grant application
- Average length of time to receive a planned gift
- Average length of time to deliver a service, per service provider

Customer Indicators

- Number of clients treated by hour, day, week, month, quarter, or year
- Average $ per donor ($)
- Collection rates (%)
- Average collection time (# days)

Learning and Growth

- Employee turnover (#)
- Certification levels (%)
- Time in training (#)
- Average absenteeism (#)
- Per capita annual cost of training ($)

Please note that *absolutely none of these* has anything whatsoever to do with making progress on the problems non-profits were created to solve! If you take out the word "gift" and "donor" and substitute "price" and "client" we could be talking about any Microsoft or Hertz or PepsiCo.

When I was younger I thought non-profits were unquestionably wonderful. Who wouldn't want a life filled with meaning, spent in the company of others who felt the same way? I thought non-profits were almost sacred, removed from that nasty profit motive. Then I had an epiphany and started thinking about the money. Where did it come from and go to? I learned that there is no "clean" money. While non-profits are, by definition, a step removed from pure capitalism designed to create profits for owners, they depend on those who have been successful capitalists to survive. Without somebody out there willing to charge more for their goods and services than it costs them to make and sell them, there would be no non-profit sector at all! Yet non-profits perpetrate the mirage of "holier-than-thouism," much like revirginization operations. Once I discovered the "wizard" pulling the levers, things got pretty interesting.

Fascinated by the dichotomy between truth and image, and drawn to the quest to close the gap between rich people and poor people, I spent much of my early career trying to get paid to write and help execute development plans for non-profits. Pretty soon I became frightened by the prevalence of community-based grassroots non-profits who got their money from a few rich people. My concept was that the money should be a mirror image of the point of the organization. Instead, what I found was that only a very few executive directors were really interested in asking themselves whether the people they were "serving" were giving back to the organization's well-being, if not in time then in money. They had a lot of trouble understanding that development planning was neither fundraising nor accounting, but instead a higher-order strategic dose of tough love.

Why? Because they were too enamored of their mission. How could anyone argue against helping refugees survive displaced person camps? Or deny that teenage runaways need a safe place to stay? Or that caregivers for incapacitated elderly need respite care?

Running a successful non-profit starts by *ignoring the organization's mission,* un-memorizing press releases, and deleting all boilerplate on grant applications. I am a big fan of the hit TV series *What Not To Wear.* In it, Stacey and Clinton - whom I will describe with only two words: *totally awesome* - offer their client a trade-off: take a VISA card with $5,000 on it and shop with them in NYC - but only if they agree to throw away whatever Stacey and Clinton order them to. People do not change unless they have to. Being naked is a strong motivator.

The first step in successful non-profit management is to toss every single thing in one's proverbial closet. Get rid of the smug pantsuits, the down-at-the-heel boots, and the slightly pathetic polyester.

This will put you smack up against the vested interests

of the Board, who are the ones who filled the closet in the first place. You, the Director, will be staking your reputation and livelihood on being able to refill it with stuff that actually suits your body type. The goal is to make the inside match the outside. Organizational behavior must reflect the mission. So let's take a hard look in the closet. We'll assess governance, money operations, programs, and people.

Governance is basically who gets to tell people what to do. My rule of thumb is that if the programmatic beneficiaries do not make up at least one-third of the Board (and I'd like it to be half), the organization is perpetuating a culture of patronization. I once did a study of community-based loan funds. These were organizations which lent poor people money to better themselves. I concluded that, while the raising of loan funds was a good idea, the money would go further by eliminating the do-gooder middlemen and just handing it out to the poor people so they could do with it what they would.

Governing an improv troupe is a very risky business. Since it's all about "group mind," all decisions have to be made by consensus, and there's no operating manual on what decisions have to be made. Our group has had to decide where, when, and how often to perform, who we want to coach us, when we want to practice, and how much we will all kick in. We're tiptoeing around a decision about how to develop an audience - and who will step up and do the work. We are also approaching decisions on whom we want to ask to join us. Someday we'll probably have to decide whether to ask someone to un-join.

Bearing in mind that money is only one resource, a sound non-profit is one that gets at least a third of its juice from those who benefit from the fact that it exists. It hurts my property values to have a homeless guy rapping on drivers' side windows at my corner. So it is in my economic self-interest to contribute to the homeless shelter two blocks away. The parents of the kids in the tutoring program I volunteer for can bring snacks, pass out flyers, or speak at recruiting sessions. The kids can decorate the brochure. The goal is expanding our definition of economic self-interest.

The actual money should come from at least three different sources, fairly evenly distributed. We know in improv that three is kind of a magic number. The three-legged stool is more stable that the four-legged chair. I've seen lots of non-profits get a big grant – and speedily fail as soon as the grant runs out.

All of the three sources should benefit from the fact that the non-profit exists, though they can be one or two steps removed from directly receiving goods or services. Most immediately, those who benefit should contribute in time or money. Those in the neighborhood or allied in the same field (e.g., local businesses who hire graduates from the schools, or other tutoring organizations) care that the non-profit exists and benefit from its success, so they should also kick in. The final third can come from a more-removed organization or government agency.

Financial decisions in improv sadly reflect a starving artist context. There is a well-deserved fear of closing doors to talented people who don't have much income, and a wariness to embrace the idea that you get what you pay for. Theater operations notoriously lose money, whether they are our little facility or legendary Broadway houses. Hardly any improv actors get paid, even a little.

When I decided to co-found a troupe, we started with an intensive series of master classes. My partner and I recruited teachers, designed the curriculum, secured the venues, did all the marketing – then we threw ourselves into becoming students like everyone else. Along the way we experimented with methods to recruit attendees. I wanted to hold auditions and charge a little money for the opportunity to receive a detailed evaluation from our instructors. Most auditions end in…dead air. No thank you, no reasons why you didn't make it. Just silence. This tone reinforces the worst aspects of elitism, and shows zero regard for people's feelings. You lay it all out there. The air is thick with fears of rejection. You're competing against everybody there, yet success in improv is based on making others look good. You have to be relaxed yet focused, not care and care, think hard and not think at all. It is well nigh impossible.

In contrast, we wanted to begin our endeavor with a tone of respectful feedback and transparency. We wanted to take the people we thought were the most open and connected. We were hoping to model that you get what you pay for. But both the idea of auditions, and the idea of charging for the opportunity to participate in same, feedback or no, turned out to be a non-starter. It was too far from the prevailing culture to be viable.

Operational metrics like the ones we tried are the hardest to make work. Every single detail has to tell the organization's unique story. When I was on the Board of a local theater company I was routinely invited to presentations on lighting, set design, costumes and sound. I learned that each discipline, on its own, must reflect the tone and plot of the play it is designed to enhance. Imagine *Romeo and Juliet* told only through props, or *West Side Story* through lighting cues.

Even something as straightforward as location location location can reinforce a non-profit's raison d'etre or detract from it. Is an anti-poverty program located in a poor neighborhood? A tutoring program in the same school district as the schools it serves? A theater school near where many actors live or work? I had a pointed argument with a friend of mine who worked to develop low-income housing and chose to live in an upper class suburb.

Who is answering the phone? What is on the walls? Filling the air with sound? I recently visited a world-renowned organization dedicated to social entrepreneurship. Absolutely nothing about their physical presence reflected their mission. This amazing venture could have been any of the law firms, PR consultants, or rent-a-set-of-cubicles typically found in a high-rise above a Metro stop.

Running an improv troupe involves communications, marketing, performance standards, hiring (and maybe firing). All of these details must reflect the group's unique culture. Originally we wanted to attract performers from other disciplines. We sought dancers, musicians, story tellers. To reflect this tone we had a balloon artist decorate our organizational meeting, and had a great guitarist perform as people were coming into the building. You could hear him sing and play all the way down the hall, practically to the sidewalk. He even wrote a song for us.

Programmatic goals define what the organization actually does. Tutoring, delivering blood to war zones, lobbying for gay rights are programs for sure, but goals are needed. How many kids read at a higher grade level after tutoring than before? Did blood help save lives? Was pro-gay legislation passed or anti-gay legislation killed or muted? These are programmatic goals. Here's the paradox: the goals don't have to be distinctive, but the combination of operational activities, the web of interconnectedness which makes them real - the infrastucture - does.

After money, infrastructure decisions tell more about the health of a non-profit than anything else. This is because infrastructure costs big bucks, lasts a while, and obviates alternatives. Put another way, if an organization is willing to invest in infrastructure - no matter what they buy - they generally have a higher tolerance for risk. In my book that translates to courage.

People, paid and unpaid, are the face of the organization. As such, I think that Boards and staff should reflect the one-third, one-third, one-third financial structure described earlier. Our tutoring organization, serving exclusively low-income black and Hispanic children, is 99% white and college-educated. This isn't good. The inside doesn't match the outside.

In improv, our cast is all we have. We're trying to produce comedy based on connection, to represent on the stage our vision of real life the way it is supposed to be. Putting out this message has resulted in a cast that is much, much, much more diverse than the typical improv troupe. We're older and more physically different, with a mix of improv and non-improv backgrounds. We're also probably weirder (in a good way) than most, but I can't say that for sure. If we had been "successful" in more traditional troupes we would not have needed to found our own!

Still, the experience of founding and trying to run a successful improv troupe, much like that of guiding a non-profit, can only work when the shroud of pretense is lifted and intellectual laziness is burned away. There is no "clean" money. Glamorizing impoverishment for art is fundamentally self-defeating. That is not to say that the journey is not worth taking. As long as there are goals!

Chapter Nine

Ten Things You Need To Know To Look Smart About Money

Let's face it. Being financially smart is sexy – provided you're not a jerk about it. This book is written on the presumption that more is not better, but dumb is stupid. Finance is one area where if you don't get it, it gets *you*.

Looking smart and being smart are two different things, but for the many people who have to fake it till they make it, this chapter is for you. And my not-so-secret hope is that you'll like looking smart so much that you'll end up actually *being* smart. Sort of like the fact that it takes as much energy to cheat successfully on a test as it does to learn the material in the first place... .

Some of the things I want to teach you here are straight-up math, and some are more conceptual. Feel free to skip around as the whim strikes you.

For me, finance came in my twenties, and it was a decision, not a calling. My father was in the rag trade, working for a high-end department store. I grew up reading *Women's Wear Daily*, which I spread out on our living room floor. Sprawled on my belly so I was lying on the heating register, I pored over that thing, hunting for secrets about what it meant to be out in the world. Wearing killer shoes.

The decision to make my living in finance happened when two things occurred simultaneously. First, I saw many of my friends starting little non-profits, small co-ops, and creative ventures. They all got hung up on the money part. Second, I realized that the oppressions that most directly affected me, anti-Semitism and sexism, came with financial stereotypes. Jews were supposed to be scheming penny-pinchers - but annoyingly useful because we take risks. Women, at least when I was growing up, were supposed to be ecstatic at spending but not so happy about earning. As for me, I didn't faint at the sight of a number so I decided to take a shot. Now it's your turn to understand:

1. *What is the best way to pay off your credit cards?*

Depending upon why you got into credit card debt in the first place, paying off the cards may or may not be a good idea. Assuming you were buying expensive things you might not really need (and you took the tags off), use your savings first. But those savings are for emergencies, you say! Too much credit card debt *is* an emergency. There are credit cards out there charging over 20% interest for cash advances!

Most people who have decided to pay off their cards (thereby abdicating their role in propping up our economic system, two-thirds of which is based on consumer purchases) line up the statements and choose to pay off the smallest balance first, then the next smallest balance, and so on. They do this because it is so satisfying to pay off even a single balance and cut up the cards, one by one.

However, this method is completely wrong. Sorry. Don't mean to be a killjoy, but the correct thing to do is to line up the statements based on the Annual Percentage Rate (APR) that each card charges. All payments should go to reduce the card that carries the highest APR, even if it takes a loooong tiiiiime to completely pay it off. The next-highest charging card should be next, and so on.

2. ***What's the Dow and why should you care?***

You should care about the Dow and how it works because it is a stand-in for the performance of the US economy. Critics say it unfairly skews analysis towards the "big kids" and ignores smaller companies which play a pivotal role in job creation. In my opinion, caring about the Dow is like watching the Oscars on TV. Even though I have never owned an evening dress in my entire life, I want to see what the stars are wearing because it affects what I'll find at the mall.

The Dow stands for the Dow Jones Industrial Average. It is a list of thirty stocks that are supposed to represent a microcosm of the U.S. economy. The Average, or Index, was created by *Wall Street Journal* co-founder Charles Dow and his statistician, Edward Jones, in 1896. It originally had twelve stocks, which really were industrial. Now many stocks in the index, like Microsoft, have nothing whatever to do with heavy industry.

The Dow is calculated by taking the per-share price of the thirty stocks which comprise it and dividing by a magic number which is currently 0.132319125. Presently, every one-dollar change in price in a particular stock within the average equates to a 7.56 (1/0.132319125) point movement.

3. *How to Do a Percent Change Calculation*

High on my list of ways to look smart is the ability to do a percent change calculation. These helpful puppies let us determine how fast or slowly one thing changed vs. another. This is so we can make guesses about the most fun part of finance, which is linkage and relationships. How fast do housing costs rise relative to income? Does cutting the price of cars make people buy more higher-end brands? Does raising the minimum wage help or hurt unemployment? Percent change calculations work because they relate changes of vastly different magnitudes. And it's the math fact that nobody remembers, so once you learn it you're golden.

To calculate the percent change, you need two numbers for the same fact, one from the most recent time period and one from another time period in the past. Say the number of books sold last year was 10,000 vs. the number sold this year, which was 20,000. We subtract one number from another (I am sure you figured that out!), then take the result (10,000) and divide it by LAST YEAR. One hundred percent increase, people! Not too shabby!

Books sold last year:	10,000
Books sold this year:	20,000
Difference:	10,000
% Change:	10,000/10,000 = 100%

Now let's look at what happens when this year's numbers are *lower* than last year's. Take my weight this year vs. my weight last year. Not so fast! I'm not revealing *those* numbers. Okay, how about my heating bill after installing energy-efficient windows.

This year's heating bill:		$500
Last year's heating bill:		$600
Difference:		($100)
% Change:	$100/$600 =	(16.6%)

Many people know to subtract one number from another just fine, but then they divide by the most recent year. That's wrong because the point of a percent change calculation is to figure out whether the bill is bigger or smaller than the year we started with.

$$\frac{\text{Last Year's Bill} - \text{This Year's Bill}}{\text{Last Year's Bill}}$$

4. *How Does Social Security Work?*

"Social Security"– that's a great name for an improv group!

Most people think Social Security is a sort of enforced savings program where you pay money in while you're working and the government kindly holds onto it in your own private account. When you retire they, again very kindly, give some of it back every month until you die. *Wrong.*

In Social Security, as in improv, you don't get back what you put in. You might get more, or, more likely, less. No one is supposed to be counting.

Our improv troupe is about six months old. None of us has ever been in a troupe before, and we just don't know what we don't know. In the beginning, we just threw ourselves into it, grateful for an outlet, proud to have created one. Now we have an interesting problem - some of us are putting in more, a lot more, than others. Those with a high work rate are, not surprisingly, improving rather dramatically. Those who aren't coming to rehearsal are not. While it is always a good challenge to make one's scene partner look good, no matter who they are, none of us is skilled enough to know what to do when our scene partners do the totally wrong thing. Over and over. Since I am the initial organizer of the troupe, people look to me for guidance. Some are starting to complain about one person in particular, who basically wrecks every scene they are in.

So we've now established a norm that, barring pre-arranged or extenuating circumstances, if you don't come to rehearsal you can't perform that week. We're trying to make sure people get enough out of participation to make them want to continue to play. Not an even exchange, but good enough.

Improv is based completely on the concept of giving and receiving gifts, which can never be refused. Denying your scene partner's offer is always, always a "no no." Instead, the good improviser finds a way to accept. Over-accepting, which is adding to the gift and passing it on, is usually very funny.

In his book *The Gift*, Lewis Hyde explains the difference between a gift and a commodity. Gifts are never intended to line the nest of the recipient. They are to be enjoyed, rejoiced in, then augmented and passed on. Not necessarily the same plate of home-made brownies, but a similar substitute. He gives example after example of how anybody who tries to profit from a gift gets punished.

Interestingly, according to Hyde, gifts, although they cannot be commoditized, have very definite values - values which are scaldingly clear to both the giver and the receiver. Anyone who's gotten a secret Santa offering below the stated amount can weigh in on this. For years my mother sent size ten clothing to my size six address. I took the point.

Social Security works on the same basic principle that everyone gives and everyone takes, and the payments are treated as gifts and not commodities. Some people take more than they give, others the opposite. The first monthly Social Security payment was issued on January 31, 1940 to Ida May Fuller of Ludlow, Vermont. In 1937, 1938, and 1939 she paid a total of $24.75 into the Social Security System. Her first check was for $22.54. After her second check, Fuller already had received more than she contributed over the three-year period. She lived to be a hundred and collected a total of $22,888.92.

Regardless of how much we pay or how much we get, all Americans are in the Social Security boat together. Hence the idea that Social Security is a massive intergenerational "social contract." During the Great Depression, the United States decided to protect some of its old people from starving to death. Fifty percent of the elderly were impoverished, so starvation was a real possibility. Roosevelt got the legislation, originally known as the Federal Old Age and Survivors and Disability Insurance Act, passed in 1935.

People with jobs pay 6.2% of their salary into a pot every year that they work. (As of this writing, President Obama is talking about lowering this payroll tax to 4.2%.) Their employer also pays 6.2%. Once someone's salary hits $106,800 they're done paying for the year. So if I earn that, or $1.6 million, I pay the same amount. Starting at age sixty-two, all Americans who have worked at least eight years in their lives can start to take out up to $2,346 each month, until they die. The longer they wait to start taking money out, the more per month they can hit up the government for. Like many things in finance, this is a game of chicken.

Chicken? Yes. It's us vs. Uncle Sam. What can go wrong, you ask? First, you could die. All the money you put in stays in the gift pot for somebody else. Second, but not very likely, the pot could run dry.

On my latest Social Security statement I was thoughtfully informed that the Social Security system could run out of money in 2046. But it won't really. Even using the most frightening assumptions (all the young people eschew paid employment) I'll get three-quarters of what I am counting on. Much more likely, given that Social Security is considered the "third rail" of American politics (touch it and you get electrocuted), Congress will raise the payroll contributions of those young(er) people who are contributing, and I'll get my money.

5. *What's an APR versus an interest rate?*

First of all, APR stands for "Annual Percentage Rate." It's a component of most debt you incur. But we're not done. Anybody with a credit card has been teased by this one. Knowing what it is, really, can score you street cred, and save you lots and lots of money on long-term loans like mortgages.

Earlier this year I refinanced my house. I went to a credit union on my corner because a) I believe in credit unions and b) it was on my corner. I wanted an interest rate lower than 5%, and I found one: 4.25%. But the APR was 5.2%. Since this loan advertised no closing costs, I was suspicious of hidden fees. Because I knew what an APR was. And I was right, there were some hidden costs - for the appraisal mainly.

The APR is a compilation of all the fees you'll ever pay over the life of the loan, brought into today's world. It's a sort of time machine for your money. When you get a loan there will be closing costs, regardless of what the bank tells you. Somebody has to pay the appraiser and make sure you really own the house. When you get a credit card, there may be annual fees.

The APR is a mini-internal rate of return calculation. If you don't want to know this, just take a short mental vacation now... *ahhh... I am shopping at the Eileen Fisher Outlet in Secaucus. Cashmere in size PS. Tax free plus discounts...sheer heaven...*Internal rate of return calculations bring all the plusses and all the minuses back to today. Like the time machine I mentioned earlier. Because we can't know the future, we have to make assumptions. How high will inflation be? What's the likelihood that any given bill won't be paid? How much do you trust the borrower? These answers combine to form what's called the "present value interest factor." It is used in every APR.

APRs are always higher than stated interest rates because they include fees and charges. Quoting an interest rate alone is misleading, very baitish and switchish. However, unless you always pay your loan or credit card balance in full by the due date, all APRs are not created equal. Depending upon when the interest charges are compounded, the same stated APR can result in paying almost 10% more than the bank originally told you. This is because the bank is collecting interest on the interest they are charging you.

As Albert Einstein said, "The most powerful force in the universe is compound interest." Obviously, the more frequently the interest compounds, the more interest on the interest on the interest you pay.

6. What's the difference between the debt and the deficit?

Lots and lots of people are confused about the difference between the debt and the deficit. The words sound a lot alike and both sound scary. To make things worse, they affect and are affected by one another.

The debt is how much is owed as of right now. It's the

accumulation of all the money that's been borrowed that has not been repaid. Virtually every person, and every country, has debt. The deficit is the difference that happens when the amount of current money coming in is not big enough to cover the amount of current money going out. As deficits accumulate they add to the debt. Both debts and deficits can be good or bad; we'll talk about that a little later.

As I write this, the United States owes about $13,849,257,000,000. I put those six zeros in there at the end because I couldn't type fast enough to get any one number exactly right. (Look up the US National Debt Clock: Real Time.) This means that our government borrowed close to $14 trillion dollars and we haven't paid it back. This nearly $14 trillion translates into about $178,000 per citizen.

Be aware that this $14 trillion is what the government is in hock for - not what we personally have borrowed and not yet repaid. That number, which includes credit cards, mortgage loans, and consumer debt, is $52,135 per person.

The deficit, remember, is the difference between current insies (technical term, like that used for belly buttons) and current outsies. That number is about $1.3 trillion. Every time you receive a paycheck and groan over how much your employer withholds for taxes, you make this number smaller. Every time the FBI protects you from somebody who went postal, the deficit gets bigger.

So now the fun question: are debts and deficits good

or bad? The answer is, "Yes."

If our government didn't owe people, primarily China and Japan, our ability to run the county day-to-day would be severely hampered. Think about what would happen if you had no credit cards, car loans, or mortgages. Then ponder what happens to retail stores, car manufacturers, and home builders. Not to mention realtors, bankers, makers of window treatments, and landscaping companies.

At the same time, owing governments, or people, upsets the balance of power. Hence the term, "in debt." In German, the word for debt, *schuld*, is the same as the word for "guilt." It is very hard, for example, for the United States to chastise China for human rights violations when we need their money to pay the very salaries of those righteous chastisers.

Most of us carry some level of debt - it would be virtually impossible to buy assets without it. Deficits, on the other hand, can be very dangerous. In simple terms, deficits are when you spend more money day to day than you take it. They tend to happen when we're not paying attention, living in a dream world, or run into some serious trouble.

It is very, very easy to simply not pay attention.

What's that joke? I know I still have money because my checkbook still has checks? Some days I just do not go into a store because I am afraid I will be seduced by what looks in the moment like the deal of a lifetime. Same reason Kool Whip Lite is as far as I go in the sweets department. (My children had sugar-free Jello cake for their birthday parties until they were old enough to stage a protest.)

Living in a dream world happens when perfectly capable adults lose the ability to add and subtract. We feel entitled to standards of living that we can't afford. Or we fall for the bait-and-switch. Take water heaters. The GE Geospring is priced at about $1,700 but it costs about $300 a year to operate. Whirlpool's heater is the same size, with a sticker price of $337. That puppy costs $520 a year to run. Water heaters can last twenty years, so the Geospring will cost $6,000 to run plus the original $1,700, or $7,700. The Whirlpool will cost $10,400 to run, plus the original $337, or $10,737. Buying the fancier water heater, is, in addition to the environmental benefits, a much better deal.

Guess what? More people buy the Whirlpool. They simply do not want to face the reality of the impact of their decisions, or admit they fell for the ol' bait and switch.

My husband is a personal bankruptcy lawyer who sees first-hand what happens when people, some of whom have the above problems and some of whom don't, run into trouble. Most bankruptcies happen because of health, employment, or marital crises, which tend to combine and re-combine in particularly wrenching ways.

In the US, bankruptcy is (currently) viewed as a second chance. When I was growing up, "bankruptcy" was one of those words like "divorce" and "cancer" uttered in whispered tones while glancing over your shoulder to make sure the person you were talking about was out of ear-shot.

In bankruptcy, some of one's debts are eligible for forgiveness. If you file the kind of bankruptcy (Chapter 7) that causes you to sell all your non-exempt stuff, you get 100% debt forgiveness. While it differs from state to state, most bankrupt people who have property to protect (they file under Chapter 13 of the Bankruptcy Code) pay about ten cents on the dollar to the people they owe money to. Lest you think this is a breeze, over seven in ten Chapter 13 bankruptcies fail, which means that legal protection ends and creditors can declare open season.

We deal with debts and deficits in improv too. The point of having a troupe rather than a random accumulation of players coming together to perform and then going their separate ways, is because, in any one instant, some players are creating a surplus and others are creating a deficit. Everybody has great performances, where you feel the flow. The character you are playing just understands what to do. It's like the story is written and you know your part.

One time I was playing a passive-aggressive husband, whose wife wanted him to finish the "honey do" projects around the house. I'd constructed the most convoluted set of (invisible) kitchen cabinetry possible and left it all spread out in a weird shape on the floor. Then sat down in one corner of the stage and refused to budge. My "wife" got more and more frustrated, then eventually crossed the stage in front of my contraption to get to the phone to (horror of horrors) call my mother to complain. Clearly, I had to stop her. So I got up and, without thinking for one second, circumnavigated my way around, over, and between the imaginary cabinets to block her access to the phone. The audience roared, because I had given not a hint that I knew the cabinets were still all over the floor, much less their exact dimensions. That was a great example of "the flow."

Every improviser also experiences the "anti-flow." Probably my worst scene was in a class on Patterns and Games, which I liked and generally did well in. For some unknown reason I decided to play a character who shamed and humiliated her scene partners. That in itself would not have been so bad, given that I have trouble playing high-status characters. But I decided to exert my power by ordering my poor scene partner around, making him bark like a dog, kiss my feet, and generally grovel. Of course, because improv is based on agreement, he complied. This went on for a disturbing amount of time and was a really novice move.

In the first scene, I created a surplus for myself and my troupe. The audience was impressed and filled with delight. In the "be my dog" scene, I used up a ton of good will and definitely ended up in a deep deficit-y hole.

We have troupes so we can, hopefully, balance one another out. While each of us has short-term (hopefully) deficits from time to time, none of us wants to carry a long-term debt. When the debt gets too big, we either have to make a decision to forgive it, or "detroupify" one of our members.

Occasionally, countries grant one another "debt forgiveness." Surprisingly, this can be but doesn't have to be based on financial reasons alone, or even on why the debt was incurred in the first place.

In late December 2005, the Board of the International Monetary Fund (an organization created to lend money) approved 100% debt forgiveness, totaling $3.3 billion for a whole host of countries, except Mauritania, which was faulted for its poor economic management. Two other countries, Cambodia and Tajikistan, also qualified.

But not all the countries who got debt forgiveness wanted it. Uganda's President, Yoweri Museveni, said that canceling the debt is not the solution to poverty: "I am grateful that the G-8 (rich countries which advise and help fund the IMF) cancelled our debt, but this is just a relief but not the solution, because if you cancel a poor man's debt without giving him a source of money, he will contract another debt."

Debt forgiveness, understandably, also has a "crowding out" effect on new lending. Other than transaction fees and often high interest for awhile, who wants to lend money when there's a low likelihood it will be paid back? Ever...

By the same token, our improv troupe will have a debt vs. deficit decision to make soon. We have definitely forgiven debt, but it has not worked to create a source of resources, just as Mr. Museveni warned.

7. What is the balance of trade?

It shows how much a country imports vs. exports. Next time you go shopping for clothes, look at the tag inside the collar and see where the item was made. Odds are nearly fifty-fifty it was made in China. Chinese apparel is flooding the US, and has been for awhile. Between June 2004 and June 2005, the amount of clothing coming from China to US ports grew 99%! Our biggest exports are probably computers and corn. As of this writing, we're in the hole almost $46.3 billion, but the hole is shrinking as the US sends more industrial supplies to, you guessed it, China.

I like thinking about the balance of trade because it is something I can directly affect, unlike other things like inflation, deflation, job creation, and the value of the dollar.

Opinion differs on whether a trade deficit (we import more than we export) is good or bad. Proponents of the "good" theory sing "We Are the World" waaay too much. They also like the low prices of goods made by workers who are paid thirty cents an hour. Proponents of the "bad" theory talk about oil dependency and isolationism. They say we should save American jobs by making and buying all of our goods at home.

8. Are tax refunds bad?

Despite how much fun it is to get a big check from Uncle Sam just in time for Spring Sales, tax refunds are bad. First, a big refund means that you've let the government hold onto your overpayments for up to a year, interest free. Sadly, many of the same people who do this run up big credit card bills in the meantime! Second, most people get all excited and blow the refund check on something they don't really need, then start the over-withholding all over again. Third, over-withholders do so because they either aren't paying attention or they don't trust themselves with the money, and that's the biggest problem of all.

9. *What does the Federal Reserve Do?*

Another great name for a troupe, by the way...
To answer this question, we have to ask ourselves, "What is the point of government?" Be you a queen, a pharaoh, a dictator, or a President, one of the first answers will be "to get money and spend it on stuff." The Federal Reserve, also known as the Nation's Central Bank, decides how much money there will be. They do this by:

- Causing the printing of said money (literally).
- Buying back United States' government bonds.
- Setting the interest rate at which banks can borrow from the mothership.

The Fed's overall objective is to keep the money flowing and prevent panic.

But the United States did not have a Federal Reserve until 1913. Before that there were two attempts at centralizing our monetary system, one by President

Madison and one by President Jackson. Both failed because detractors did not want anyone to control what counted as money (earlier bills were called "Continentals" after the Continental Congress, which issued them) or tell them what to do with theirs. Fighting over who has the right to tell who else what to do with their money happens all over the world. It's the reason that England doesn't use the Euro. The Brits don't take direction from anybody. Period.

Control is political. Because whenever you have money you have politics, and vice-versa, the Federal Reserve is "independent within the government." The President appoints its head, currently Ben Bernanke, for a four-year term, which always spans Presidential election years. He is the head of a small Board of Governors, who serve for fourteen years.

Mr. Bernanke's decisions affect how much money your bank has to lend and the rate at which they get it in the store in the first place. To some degree, his actions also affect whether you even have a job, because the Fed operates the cheap money spigot your employer takes his pail to in order to fund expansion and day-to-day operations. The supermarket's prices for Granny Smith apples are affected by the Fed because its policies affect how much the grocery store's dollars are worth in Australia. In fact, it is hard to find something in our financial lives that Mr. Bernanke does not have his fingers in.

Nevertheless, he is not a magician. He doesn't control what Congress or the President does. He can't keep the stock market from panicking, purses from closing, or your employer from firing you. Most importantly, he cannot tell you what to do, or not to do, with your own money.

10. Whom should you trust?

My answer is, and I say this without bitterness: no one but yourself. Would you trust someone else to run your sex life? Finance is absolutely as personal and, some would argue, a lot more important. Like sex, finance spans the full range of human emotion. Also like sex, nobody else can decide what will make you happy, although whole industries exist to try.

So I say, like Henny Youngman, *"Take my financial planner. Please."*

There is no one who knows what you need to do with your money better than you do. While there is a role for experts (e.g., tax advisors) be afraid, be very afraid, of anybody who purports to:

- Make you rich.
- Buy, sell, or save your house.
- Get you a job.
- Do any of these things quickly.

Not everyone is a crook. I'm not saying that. *But they cannot possibly really care.* Brokers make money even if you don't. So do your mutual fund advisors, your bankers, your realtors, and your financial planners. Even book publishers and me!

The follow-up question is, should you trust yourself?

Only you know your values, secret desires, biggest mistakes, and day-to-day modus operandi. Since there is no right answer when it comes to any of the most basic questions of financial security (although there are guidelines, facts, and skills or I wouldn't be writing this book), the key job is to make the inside match the outside. Money and strategy are two sides of the same coin.

In improv, trust is paramount. The question of whom to offer it to is fascinating. There is a fundamental conflict involved if you, like me, believe that the point of improv is to unlock creative genius. Everybody can do improv, because we're all doing it every day of our lives. The question is, should everybody be allowed to charge money for it on the stage?

In Chicago, improvisational heaven, students who complete the Level 5B curriculum at Improv Olympics (having spent $1,820 and attended fifty-six three-hour classes) get six to eight weeks of stage time with their class. They perform on Sunday nights. (By the way, Improv Olympics has been called "iO" since they were sued by the "real" Olympics.)

There is a mysterious group of secret agents who scout these Sunday night talentfests and choose people in them to be on one of (currently 31) iO-sponsored teams. The teams are allowed to live for a few months. Then they are either killed, revived, or picked apart. The secret agents are part of existing teams, and their methods are, well, secret.

If someone does make a house team they can perform...

for free...as long as the team fills seats, which run from free to $14 per. Once in a while a performer is selected for The Big Time, which can mean *Saturday Night Live* or *MadTV*. Given that there are about 25 shows a week, with ten performers each, the chances of making it big are infinitesimally small.

So why do people move to Chicago to do improv? Because, in part, they are hooked on the feeling of trust in one's scene partners and in oneself.

But what about mistakes, you might ask. How can I trust myself when I screw up big time? I believe that in finance, as in improv, *mistakes are good.*

Read any bio of a gazillionaire and they will tell you about how they lost a boatload of money, only to regain even more (sort of like being on a diet). Skilled improvisers use every part of the buffalo to bring the funny. Often the "mistakes" are the best part. In one performance I was in, my character pushed people away. I hadn't meant to do this literally, but my hands did things that my head had not asked them to. The audience laughed. So next time I did it again. And they laughed again. Mistake, yes. Bad, no!

The trick with finance, and with improv, is to make a lot of mistakes. Just do it on purpose, because you are reaching for something good. Having my hands do something that my head said no to is an excellent behavior for an improviser. Taking a risk with your money is bound to turn out well long-term, regardless of the short-term consequences, because you will have learned how and when to take risks. But I want *you* to be the one making the decisions, not outsourcing them to somebody else.

Afterword

You know what robbers say in the movies, "Your money or your life!" Well, from a certain perspective, your money is your life. It's not the most important thing, for sure, but inarguably an essential resource. And the way you get it, spend it, waste it, and give it away is a reflection of who you are and what you stand for. Good thing Hummers have been discontinued....

Take a look around. Where you sit, what you sit in, what you're wearing and who is there beside you are all affected by your financial choices, conscious or not. My goal is to make you want to be conscious.

I don't ask that you be unafraid. I'm definitely afraid, and the more I think about it the more scared I become. But, if it's any comfort, nobody knows what they're doing. Not you, not Wall Street, not the good people at the International Monetary Fund. Everyone is making their best guesses, based on assumptions and knowledge. Like improvisers, they're making it up as they go along.

Hopefully, you feel more confident about quantifying your assumptions and have more knowledge to help you do so. You know that cars can kill, and not just while you're driving. You get that when the Dow goes up or down, the companies listed on it don't make or lose money. You know the difference between asset utilization, revenue, profit, and cash flow, and the importance of using any one of these concepts to define "good." You know that buying on sale always causes money to leave your pocket.

And you see the impact of your decisions on everybody else, and the impact of their decisions on you.

Improvisational comedy works on the same basic principle: we are all connected, and the more we embrace this sometimes uncomfortable fact, the funnier things get. Paradoxically, this makes it even more important that each actor on the stage need something really badly, and express that need as strongly as possible.

We all need money. But more isn't necessarily better, nor is less. You're not stupid if you're not rich. You are at a disadvantage if you're not scared, and even more out to sea if you withhold your trust.

So trust yourself, first. Waste money on purpose. Wear art. Eat well. Fail spectacularly. Maybe even go see some improv.

About the Author

Laurie R. Kauffman has a Masters with Highest Honors in Finance, and is a former stockbroker and local public radio personality. She founded Net Worth Consulting, Inc. in 1983 to help her corporate and non-profit clients connect money to value. In 2010 she co-founded Third Beat, an improv training program and performance troupe.

Improv is harder.

Printed in Dunstable, United Kingdom

91218269R00087